Contents

Cover: A Hungarian cartoon of the
eagle of the Habsburg Empire being
entombed by nationalism
Front endpaper: One of the last
photographs of the aged Emperor
Franz Joseph taken before
his death in 1916
Rear endpaper: The Emperor Karl
visits frontline troops shortly
after his accession

Copyright © 1971: Z A B Zeman
First published 1971 by
BPC Unit 75
St Giles House 49 Poland St London W1
in the British Commonwealth and
American Heritage Press
551 Fifth Avenue New York NY 10017
in the United States of America
Library of Congress Catalogue
Card Number: 78-109172
US SBN (Cloth) 07-072798-8
US SBN (Paper) 07-072799-6

Made and printed in Great Britain by
Purnell & Sons Ltd Paulton Somerset

TWILIGHT OF THE HABSBURGS

The Collapse of the Austro-Hungarian Empire

Z A B Zeman

American Heritage Press
General Editor: John Roberts

Chapter 1
The Habsburg Inheritance

The fortunes of Europe and of the House of Habsburg were closely connected: they rose and declined simultaneously. At its height in the 16th and 17th centuries, the power of the Habsburgs spanned, apart from the central European possessions, Spain and the Low Countries. Even after Habsburg rulers had left Western Europe (they kept the Spanish Court ceremonial: it was elaborate, and reminiscent of their departed glory) their states were still extraordinarily diverse. They were inhabited by peoples who spoke at least ten different languages and who were ruled by three separate governments, and two parliaments based on the capitals of Vienna and Budapest. In the last fifty years of its existence the Empire was considered to be a great European power, but unlike Great Britain, France, or Germany, it neither possessed nor desired colonies. It consisted of highly industrialised areas which were surrounded by backward peasant holdings where time had stood still for centuries. The diversity of the Habsburg dominions brought a rich variety of political and social movements into play. It is difficult to think of an idea, of a political theory which did not have its adherents in the Empire; it was a laboratory for experiments in European history.

The Habsburg Empire sprawled away to the south and east from the centre of Europe. Its irregular frontiers extended to Lake Constance in the west, where it bordered on Switzerland, crossed the Alps into the Italian plain, and stretched far into the Balkans in the south and towards Russia in the east, reaching out into the centre of the German Empire in the north. It embraced a tremendously varied landscape. The mighty ranges of the Alps and Carpathians gave way to the gentle countryside of central Bohemia; the open plain of Hungary and eastern Galicia contrasted with the impenetrable forests of Transylvania or the stark, ragged coastline of Dalmatia. Most of the territory of the Empire lay round the River Danube, which gave it a certain geographical and economic unity.

Left: Emperor Franz Joseph, ruler of the Habsburg lands

5

RUSSIA

Prague
BOHEMIA
MORAVIA
Kraków
GALICIA

GERMAN EMPIRE
SLOVAKIA
RUTHENIA

AUSTRIA
Vienna
Budapest
BUKOVINA

YROL
STYRIA
KINGDOM OF HUNGARY
TRANSYLVANIA

ITALY
SLOVENIA
ISTRIA
CROATIA
SLAVONIA
BANAT

BOSNIA
HERZEGOVINA
RUMANIA
Bucharest

SERBIA
DALMATIA
Sarajevo
MONTENEGRO

SANJAK OF
NOVI PAZAR
BULGARIA

It had been, over the centuries, a bitterly contested area on the crossroads of civilisation and barbarism. The Turkish invasion of Christian Europe had been stopped once at Vienna in 1529 and again in 1683, and memories of centuries of battles were still alive — forbidding hilltop fortresses were a more familiar sight than elegant country houses. Despite its army and navy, its grand court, its description as a great power, it was smaller than Texas.

The distribution of peoples under the Habsburg rule, the national map of the Empire, more than matched its geographical diversity. The Slav peoples formed the majority of the population, divided by the Germans, the Magyars, and the Rumanians, who inhabited a continuous zone stretching from the west to the east in the centre of the Habsburg monarchy. Many of these peoples could look back with pride to their history in medieval times, when they had been independent nation states, so it was not surprising that national movements formed a strong undercurrent in the Empire. The Czechs in Bohemia and Moravia remembered their great national and religious leader, John Hus; later rulers, too, had struggled for recognition against the Habsburgs until the final incorporation of Bohemia with the Empire after 1620. The Hungarians had repeatedly challenged Habsburg rule; the Poles, in Galicia and the Austrian part of Silesia, had once formed a part of a powerful state of their own. In eastern Galicia the Ruthenes formed another national group closely related to the Russians.

The South Slavs — the Slovenes, the Croats, and the Serbs — also had their separate identities. They lived in Slovenia, Croatia, Slavonia, Istria and Dalmatia, and Bosnia and Herzegovina which had been occupied by the Austrian army since 1878. The Serbian states had a long history; by the end of the 7th century the Slavs had completed their occupation of the Balkan area. Croatia had first come under Hungarian rule in 1102, and after several separations and reunions was once again joined to Hungary in September 1868. The Turks conquered and incorporated the whole of Serbia with their empire in 1459; in 1463 they overran and conquered Bosnia, and in 1483 they conquered Herzegovina. In the late 19th century Serbia became virtually a satellite of Austria who also occupied Bosnia and Herzegovina.

The Habsburg Empire was especially vulnerable to the new nationalist doctrines. Halfway through the 19th century, after an unsuccessful campaign in Italy, there came the body-blow of Sadowa, inflicted on the Austrians

Top: Map showing the national composition of the territories of the Habsburg Empire (solid line). Bottom: John Sobieski, King of Poland, liberates Vienna from the Turkish siege in 1683

7

by Bismarck's Prussian army in 1866. The Habsburgs lost most of their Italian dominions and all their influence in the German states. Unification, in both Germany and Italy — the future allies of the Habsburgs — was then well on the way to completion.

Earlier than this, national revolutions had already torn the Empire almost fatally in 1848. The worst threat had come from the Hungarians. In 1867 Emperor Franz Joseph, shorn of his Italian lands, defeated in the field by the Prussians, had to yield in the famous 'Compromise of 1867'. Under it, roughly speaking, the Magyars were permitted to dominate the subject peoples of Hungary while in the other half of the new 'Dual Monarchy' the Germans were to dominate the other peoples.

The making of dualism

The Empire was thus split into two halves and the system known as 'dualism' came into being. Each half had a government and a parliament of its own. Common to both were the person of the Emperor and King (he was King in Hungary), the Ministries of Finance, Defence, and Foreign Affairs and a joint parliamentary body of equal numbers from each part. In every other regard Austria and Hungary were two separate political units. Hungary was, formally, at least, a constitutional monarchy; Austria was not. The compromise was a way out of difficulties for the Emperor, and he did not expect it to last. The Habsburgs regarded their dominions as a sacred trust put into the hands of their family, an attitude of mind which made it possible to be tough and flexible at the same time. No Habsburg ruler really expected to have to look after exactly the same possessions as his predecessor, and few of them did.

So the person of the Emperor as a link among the various Habsburg lands was immensely important. Franz Joseph I was born in 1830 and came to the throne in 1848, a year in which revolution swept Europe. Prince Metternich, who as Austria's influential foreign minister since 1809 had held together the imperial lands by his skill and diplomacy, disappeared together with his system, leaving the young emperor on a shaking throne. Franz Joseph married the beautiful Princess Elizabeth of Bavaria in 1854. When he was forced into the compromise he was still only thirty-seven and had been on the throne for nearly twenty years. In retrospect his personal life appears ill-starred. His married life soon   **13** ▷

Top: Empress Elizabeth (left), with Franz Joseph (right). Bottom: The Emperor (second from right) with his brothers. Maximilian, later the Emperor of Mexico, is on his right. Next page: Windischgrätz subdues the rising in Vienna in 1848

went wrong. His wife spent more time with horses and her Hungarian friends than with him. She led a more or less separate life until 1898, when she was assassinated by an Italian anarchist on the shore of the Lake of Geneva. Their only son, Crown Prince Rudolf, married Princess Stephanie of Belgium. He was highly critical of the way in which the Empire was ruled and was never short of plans for saving it. However, after a tragic love affair with Baroness Marie Vetsera, the two committed suicide and their bodies were found at the Mayerling hunting lodge in January 1889.

Much earlier, Franz Joseph's younger brother Maximilian had died miserably in Mexico, of which he had briefly been 'Emperor'. He arrived there in 1864, but three years later was court-martialled by rebel subjects and shot. Finally came the dynastic tragedy of 1914 when Archduke Franz Ferdinand, nephew of the Emperor and Heir Apparent since the death of Crown Prince Rudolf, was assassinated by a student revolutionary at Sarajevo in June.

Despite the sadness of his personal life, throughout his long and eventful reign the Emperor inspired loyalty, even admiration, among his subjects. Bismarck once said of him that whatever dissensions the different nationalities of Austria may have among one another 'as soon as the Emperor Joseph gets on horseback, they all follow him with enthusiasm'. The citizens of Vienna were always glad to welcome the Emperor back, even after his defeats in the field, for it was he – and not the barely existing institutional machinery of the Dual State – who truly embodied the political unity that existed within the Empire. Over the years Franz Joseph developed an impressive patriarchal personality. He possessed a certain austere – and often humourless – dignity and, although his fondness for ostentatious ceremonial was never great, nonetheless he preserved a markedly distant formality of manner even with his closest advisers. His Foreign Minister might be granted an audience of three quarters of an hour, but a delegation from the provinces might be permitted no more than five minutes. No private tragedy or public disaster ever disrupted his well-regulated life. He always attended his audiences and other appointments, and gave much of his time to general administrative duties. As senior Catholic monarch of Europe, he was a devout man and a pillar of the Church – a fact that did not, however, prevent him from a discreet variety of extramarital affairs when his wife was absent. The only liaison of any real importance was his relation-

ship with Katherine Schratt, the Burg Theatre actress who became, eventually, his lifelong companion.

Vienna, the 'Emperor's City', and capital of the Empire had, especially since the Congress of 1815, possessed a reputation for pleasure-loving gaiety, and a fondness for theatre and music—attitudes which found some exceedingly severe critics. The somewhat humourless Vienna correspondent of *The Times* before the First World War put it this way: 'Centuries of absolutist government working upon a temperament compounded of Celtic versatility, South German slackness, and Slav sensuousness, have—thanks to the constant effort of the authorities to turn attention away from public affairs and towards amusement—ended by producing a population of *dilettanti* disposed to take nothing seriously except the present pleasure. The result is depressing to those not born to the Viennese manner or capable of assimiliating the Viennese standpointlessness.' Hermann Bahr, himself a citizen of Vienna, complained that: 'Men do not lack talent but talent lacks men. Every man hides his manliness . . . Hence the terror of the Viennese when a real man appears among them. They find him uncanny and would like to hide from him—unless they be in a theatre. On the stage they know it will be over in three hours.' Adolf Hitler, who spent five years in Vienna as a young man before the First World War, came to detest it not only because it witnessed his failure and privation but also because it was a cosmopolitan town, a symbol of the Empire, where the Germans and the Czechs, the Jews and the Poles, the Magyars, and the South Slavs lived together, if not always in harmony, at least under the rule of law.

Within the lifetime of Emperor Franz Joseph, the city changed out of recognition. From a fortified city it was transformed into a modern political and commercial centre. The city walls were pulled down in 1857, and the magnificent, 187-feet-wide Ringstrasse was built in their place in the following years. In 1840, barely 500,000 people lived in Vienna; in 1910, it was the home of over 2,000,000 inhabitants. Tram lines then reached far into the new industrial suburbs in the east, near the unstable armistice line between the town and the country. The large railway terminals had been built around the mid-19th century; a few decades later, the motor car started pushing out the horse-drawn carriages including the *fiakr*, the characteristic black-lacquered cabs for hire, with their bowler-hatted drivers holding long, drooping whips. From the compact, semi-feudal town of Franz Joseph's youth, Vienna grew into a large open town

Left: A painting by Manet of the execution of Maximilian

15

with air pollution, motor accidents, cheap newspapers, weather forecasts. The same change on a smaller scale took place in the provinces giving rise to problems with which a single generation could not learn to cope.

Social order was founded on the ownership of land and on state control, a curious combination of feudalism and enlightenment, and was supported by the aristocracy, the Church, the army, and the civil service. It came under increasingly severe strain in the course of the 19th century.

As long as the Habsburg state lasted, the aristocracy managed to retain a good deal of its economic power and political influence, which extended into all spheres of life in the capital. This was at least partly due to the fact that the aristocrats still led lives luxurious enough to make money circulate fast. In the country, they lived in a way which the majority of aristocrats in other countries might have envied. At the turn of the century Prince Liechtenstein, for instance, employed an army of 1,100 gamekeepers and foresters on his Bohemian estates. Although the best of them might foster the interests of their employees, more generally the large landowners' position was that of an exclusive caste with unbending views on the social proprieties. When the beautiful Sarah, Countess of Jersey, came to Vienna in the early 1890s, she was cold-shouldered by the local aristocracy — not, apparently, because of her supposed liaison with the Prince of Wales (later Edward VII), but on account of her sleeping partnership in the Coutts bank in London.

The Austrian aristocracy was exclusive and closed to other ranks, but it usually welcomed foreigners of the same background. Foreign marriages were an important means of self-renewal, and an international bond was thus developed and maintained between the aristocratic families of Europe. Until 1918, the Austrian nobles retained a firm foothold in the diplomatic service. The remuneration for the high offices of the state was nominal, and those offices were therefore reserved for men of substance. Some of the great nobles stood in a special relationship to the throne; the Magyar, Polish, and Bohemian aristocrats usually took a greater interest in public affairs than their Austrian cousins.

However, the introduction in 1866 of compulsory military service as well as of a stiff civil service examination reduced the numbers of the nobly-born entrants. Their high and often idiosyncratic standards of personal

Top: The tragic Crown Prince Rudolf with his wife, Stephanie of Belgium (right); his mistress Marie Vetsera (left). Below: His funeral procession passes through Vienna, January 1889

honour, their indifference to the intricacies of finance and the declining value of land, tended to undermine the entrenched power of the nobility in the Habsburg monarchy. Many of its members simply gave up and lay down in the shade of the old family tree. The Emperor often preferred men of humble origins to serve him, since such men were frequently both abler and more reliable – in Franz Joseph's words, 'patriots for me'.

The officers' corps of the Austrian army was drawn largely from the middle classes, without regard to nationality. (At the Theresienstadt Military Academy, the refusal of obedience by two archdukes to their commander-in-chief in the course of the battle of Sadowa was long quoted as a warning example of insubordination.) It was described as a 'nursery of dynastic feeling'. The organization and leadership of the Imperial and Royal Army, to give it its full title, was under the exclusive control of the Emperor. Though it was frequently and sometimes ill used, it remained the mainstay of his power throughout his reign. Though it was praised by Napoleon who suffered his first defeat, at Aspern, at its hands, it was remarkably free of the spirit of militarism. Its officers were never seen, like their Prussian brothers-in-arms, sharpening their swords on the steps of the French Embassy.

Though united in its loyalty to the Emperor, the organisation of the army reflected the complexity of the Empire. The joint Austro-Hungarian army was supplemented by the *Landwehr,* or the Austrian Defence Army, and its Hungarian counterpart, the *Honvéd.* The *Landsturm* drew on all able-bodied males who were not eligible for service in any of the three bodies. It was the ultimate reserve. The joint army was administered by one of the three ministries common to both parts of the Empire, the *Kriegsministerium*, the minister being technically superior to chief-of-staff, and responsible to the Austrian and Hungarian parliamentary delegations, which had the power to approve joint military estimates. The *Landwehr,* on the other hand, was under the control of the Austrian Ministry of Defence, and there existed a similar arrangement for the *Honvéd* army. The language of command was German; the purely Ruthene, South Slav, Czech, or Polish regiments received their orders in German, but were instructed in their own language.

The Austro-Hungarian navy was mainly a coastal defence force and included a flotilla of monitors on the Danube. Its HQ was at Pola and it had, in the Bay of Kotor, an ideal base in the Adriatic. It was a match for the Russian navy, and was fast catching up with the

Right: Crowds throng one of old Vienna's great thoroughfares

Italian navy in the years before the First World War. In 1914 it had fifteen dreadnoughts. Austrian naval policy was both long-term and consistent, and navy personnel was highly disciplined. It was expected that Austria-Hungary might make a bid for the mastery of the Mediterranean.

In addition to his seventeen territorial titles, the Emperor was described as 'His Apostolic Majesty': the monarchy was the greatest Roman Catholic power in the world. At an Easter ceremony every year, the Emperor and the Empress washed the feet of the poor, in a humble imitation of Christ, under the supervision of clergy. On the feast of Corpus Christi, the Emperor joined in the clerical procession, carrying a lighted candle in his hands. Since their common victory in the course of the Counter-Reformation, the Habsburg State and the Catholic Church were bound by many invisible ties. The Church had a large stake in the wealth of the Empire. At the turn of the century, in Hungary alone, the Church with about 1,500,000 acres was the largest single landowner. Ecclesiastical art and other treasures compared favourably with those held by the House of Habsburg. Some of the great prelates commanded large incomes. (The Primate of Hungary, the Archbishop of Gran, received annually an income which was reputed to be 1,000,000 florins. Though the figure seems to be exaggerated, it was much bigger than the income of 150,000 florins—£12,500 at the value in 1890—commanded by the Archbishop of Prague.) From time to time friction occurred between Church and State, usually as a result of state control being extended to new spheres of public activity. Education was an especially sensitive topic. Despite this, the Church never ceased to maintain a close relationship with the State.

The Emperor controlled the appointments of prelates who, in turn, did not attack the State. The delicate balance between the two powerful institutions was maintained even in 1855 and again in 1870. In the former year, on his twenty-fifth birthday, the Emperor negotiated with the Church a Concordat. Besides placing primary and secondary education in large measure under Church control, it guaranteed the bishops free communication with Rome and their control over the diocesan clergy was guaranteed by the State. The Church's jurisdiction (which became even wider the following year) was again extended to a control of marriage and its property was declared inviolable. *The Times* commented on that occasion that 'a crown worn under such conditions is not worth the metal of which it is made'. Nevertheless,

Left: *The Emperor on horseback with his wife in the coach*

the changes that seemed to turn the clock back to some time before the enlightened reforms of Joseph II were more apparent than real. In any case, in 1870 the Emperor declared that the dogma of papal infallibility had made the Concordat null and void, because no contract could bind the infallible head of the Church.

The strength of the Church in the Habsburg dominions could not be put down to the protection or benevolence of the State alone. After 1848 it was argued that the Church had not been able to help to avert the revolution because for some seven decades it had been too closely linked with the State and out of touch with the people. The Jesuits were among the upholders of that view: in 1852, they began to return to the Habsburg lands.

The State stood apart, for the most part, from the public activities of the Church, and the Church, in turn, made itself as accommodating as possible. After the suicide of Crown Prince Rudolf, for example, prayers for his soul were said in Rome. The clergy in the Tyrol, on the other hand, refused to say mass, and on the day of his funeral at Botzen, despite a full church, no priest appeared, and no service was held.

The civil service of Austria-Hungary was the inheritance of reforms introduced by Joseph II at the end of the 18th century. Its critics maintained that in the second half of the 19th century it showed too much sense of authority and superiority over the people it administered, setting itself up as a caste apart; that it disliked responsibility so much that its activities had degenerated into mere form and ritual; that it was fiercely hierarchical, and resented criticism in any form. Nevertheless, Austrian civil servants were, as a rule, educated, well-mannered men who were neither cruel, nor dishonest, nor particularly stiff. Some of the territories the civil servants were responsible for, such as Bosnia Herzegovina after the occupation in 1878, thus had their first experience of modern European administration.

It was the civil service also which, more than either army or Church, reflected the political conflicts of the Habsburg Empire. It was divided by struggles concerning the widest issues of nationalism, and in particular that of language. These manifested themselves in the stiff competition, between the various peoples of the Empire, for posts in the bureaucratic hierarchy. That competition was just one of the symptoms of the growing national divisions in the last five decades of the existence of the Habsburg State. They were contained, for the time being, in an elaborate and delicate political system.

Right: Austrian soldiers remember their past glories – a monument commemorates the defeat of Napoleon I at Leipzig in 1813

Chapter 2
The Dual State

The crucial weakness of the Habsburg monarchy was always the tension between Vienna and Budapest, between the attempts to centralise emanating from the capital and the will of the Hungarians to resist those attempts. Whatever common institutions might be set up, or compromises made, nothing could alter this basic fact.

As it existed after 1867, the Hungarian part of the monarchy comprised an area of 125,609 square miles and included, apart from Hungary proper, Croatia and Slavonia, Slovakia, Transylvania, and the port and territory of Fiume (Rijeka). In 1910, on the basis of language, the Hungarians formed the largest national group, exceeding 10,000,000; the other main groups were the Germans, Slovaks, Rumanians, Croatians, and Serbians, each group numbering between 1,000,000 and 3,000,000. There were also one or two minority groups, among them the Ruthenians. Finally, there was a growing population of Jews, mainly from Galicia, who formed an increasingly apparent non-Magyar element in the population. Of the total population of over 20,000,000 more than 65 per cent depended on agriculture for their livelihood; under 20 per cent lived in the towns.

The history and language of the Hungarians combined to endow them with a strong feeling of national individuality – *'Extra Hungarium non est vita, si est vita, non est ita'* ('Outside Hungary there is no life – or if there is, it doesn't bear comparison') ran the Latin jingle. In the 9th century they penetrated the Carpathian passes from the east and settled in the plain between the Danube and the Tisza. A Turanian people, they had been responsible, under the leadership of Attila the Hun, for the third great wave of invasions which had begun to shatter the Roman Empire in the 4th century. They settled down to agriculture and horse breeding, became Christians, and went on speaking their peculiar tongue, totally different from the languages of their German and Slav neighbours.

Left: *Magyar nobles, the men who exacted recognition of their nationalist ambitions from Emperor Franz Joseph in 1867*

New invasions in the 13th century encompassed their kingdom, until in 1528 Suleiman the Magnificent forced his entry into the fortress of Buda and offered the capital to his troops to pillage. The greater part of Hungary was in the possession of the Moslem Turks and it was not until the end of the 17th and early in the 18th century that Habsburg victories cut down the extent of the Turkish power, and the Hungarians came finally under the rule of the Habsburgs.

There was serious trouble in 1848 and 1849, when the Hungarians rose against the Habsburgs, and the Croats and Rumanians against the Hungarians. In the end, the Habsburgs used the Croats as well as 200,000 Russian troops to subdue the Hungarians; when they succeeded, the new, eighteen-year-old Emperor, Franz Joseph I, had been on the throne a few months. For ten years, his rule in Hungary was absolute.

Perhaps too much has been made by historians of the fact that the Magyar civilisation had deep roots in the past. Their long history often ran very thin, as an underground stream, under foreign occupation. At the beginning of the 19th century the Hungarian language was little used by the educated, who wrote and read in Latin. But during the first half of the century, the Magyar nobility, in alliance with the small but slowly rising middle class, led a new national movement. In 1867, they achieved a political victory in the division of the Empire into Austria-Hungary; and they continued to use every method to assert their dominance over the peoples they ruled. By 1900, Hungarian was the only language used in 91 per cent of state schools.

Nevertheless, the Hungarian ruling class could be as hard on their own people as they were on the Slovaks or Rumanians or Ukrainians. (With Croatia they had concluded a compromise which resembled their own with the Habsburgs.) The Hungarian peasant, cultivator of the endless tracts of cornland, was, after 1848, no longer the personal property of the landowner. Nonetheless, he was by no means fully emancipated. The Hungarian nobility exacted an ever tougher bargain from him than from the dynasty. Apart from emigration, the peasant had little redress. Apart from the police, he hardly ever came into touch with men not of his own kind. And when he did — with the Jews or the gypsies — he usually let them know that they did not belong to the dominant race.

Top right: Hungary's steps to independence. The cruel Austrian general, Haynau, known as the 'hyena', puts down the Hungarians, 1848-49. Right: A Magyar beheads the eagle of the Dual State after 1867. Bottom: The 'fingers' of Habsburg power —the Hungarian "little" finger is the least useful and reliable

Nach thatenreichem Leben —

— ein wohlverdienter Ruhestand.

Politischer Kinderspruch.

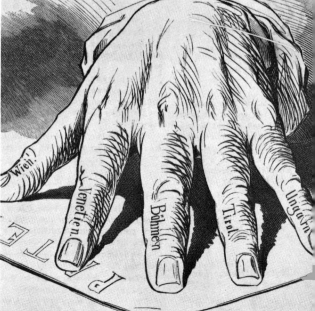

| Der schüttelt die | Der rafft sie auf. | Der trägt sie

The Austrian part of the monarchy covered an area of 115,882 square miles and included, apart from the German Austrian provinces, Bohemia, Moravia, Slovenia, Galicia, Bukovina, and Dalmatia. In 1910 the German-speaking peoples, of whom there were nearly 10,000,000, formed the largest national group. There were nearly 5,000,000 Poles; the other main groups were the Czechs, Slovenes, and Ruthenes. Finally, there were the Jews, most of whom lived in Galicia and some of whom migrated to other parts of the Empire. In spite of much social and legal assimilation they still formed a visible and distinct ethnic, religious, and sometimes linguistic group.

Of the total of over 42,000,000, 58.2 per cent of the working population in 1900 were occupied in agricultural pursuits. The figure declined sharply in the years before the war with industry absorbing the whole of the increase in population. But whereas in their own part of the monarchy the Magyars set up their own nation state, political development in Austria followed a different pattern. In the years after 1867, an intricate hierarchy of peoples was constructed with the Germans, rather insecurely, at the top.

However, they could not aspire to a position of dominance equal to that of the Hungarians in their part of the State. Hungarian was the official language in Hungary, whereas the German language did not occupy a similarly privileged position in Austria. The Austro-Hungarian banknotes were crowded, on the Austrian side, with denominations described in German, Czech, Polish, Serbian, Croat, Ukrainian, Slovak, Italian, and Rumanian. On the Hungarian side only one language was used.

The key to the system

The famous saying *'L'Autriche n'est pas un état, c'est un gouvernement'* ('Austria is not a nation, but a system of government') is the key to understanding the system. Austria's history was not the description of the blazing trail left behind by one people with one language, one literature, and one religion but the development under one government of many different peoples.

The Germans were used to playing the leading role there. They had the skills and the economic strength; as long as the Habsburgs held the titular leadership of the German Empire the supremacy of the German ruling class was rarely questioned. In the course of the Napoleonic Wars, the Habsburg ruler gave up the title of Holy Roman Emperor; in 1866 Franz Joseph lost the

Right: Franz Joseph's heir Archduke Franz Ferdinand, upholder of dynastic power, seen while hunting with his wife and child

remnants of Habsburg influence in the affairs of the German states. At the same time, Bismarck's Berlin came to compete with Vienna for the leading place among the German towns, the German language was pushed out of Hungary, and German supremacy came under severe pressure in Austria.

The Austrian Germans took their place among the peoples of Austria, and their fortunes varied with their own political skill and the favour of the Emperor. In 1878 they opposed the seizure from Turkey and subsequent legalised occupation of Bosnia Herzegovina and fell into disfavour: thirty years later, the annexation of the provinces gave them a chance to repair their error. They took it and made their agreement to the annexation known. Nevertheless, the introduction of universal suffrage in Austria in 1906 had consigned them to a position of permanent numerical inferiority. Their declining fortunes in the Habsburg monarchy, and the growth in the power of the German Empire after 1870 provoked the tensions in which the German politicians worked.

Their main competitors for power in Austria were the Czechs of Bohemia and Moravia. Like the Hungarians, the Czechs had had a long history behind them before they came under the rule of the Habsburgs. It was shaped by their relations with the Germans and by their position in the Holy Roman Empire: they were better protected than the Hungarians against the first impact of the invasions from the east. Nevertheless, it was Turkish pressure which brought about an unusual degree of cohesion in central and eastern Europe. Early in the 16th century Ferdinand Habsburg of Austria became the king of Bohemia as well as of Hungary, and the first common institutions of the then united states began to develop. When the Turkish danger subsided and the Protestant Czech estates rebelled against Habsburg rule, they were defeated at the battle of White Mountain outside Prague. In the course of the Counter-Reformation the Czechs were reconverted to Catholicism and lost their leading nobility. Early in the 19th century, Czech was a stunted language.

They had no aristocracy to lead them to national revival, but their territory possessed the resources for industrial expansion. Industrialisation implied the growth of towns and the recruitment of labour from the surrounding Czech countryside. In the 19th century, the Czechs refused the option of assuming German nationality, preferring to remain Czech. They brought their language up to date; they recaptured the towns in their own country; they formed their own middle class, which assumed the leadership of their national movement. All this would

Left: The funeral of victims of nationalist riots in Bohemia

have been impossible, or taken much longer to accomplish, had it not been for the growth of industry and commerce. It affected all the peoples in Austria-Hungary: it made the Czechs' existence as a nation possible.

The dual constitution of 1867 was a compromise worked out between the Magyar magnates and the dynasty. In the negotiations after the defeat at Sadowa, the Magyars had put forward a consistent and practicable policy. This was not, as was suspected by many Austrians, to achieve complete independence, but to gain the maximum influence in the affairs of the Habsburg Empire. When Napoleon III asked Julius Andrássy, who desired a centralised, liberal, and German Austria and a centralised, liberal, and Magyar Hungary, why Hungary had not extorted more, the answer was that, 'For us, Sir, it was not a question of asking for all we could get, but of not asking more than we could keep.'

Nevertheless, the Hungarians drove a hard bargain. They accepted everything they could get and keep in 1867 and, after that year, did not rest content. Whereas Deák and Andrássy had accepted, in 1867, that the right of the monarch to settle everything to do with the army, its leadership, command, and organisation, was constitutional, their successors did not share that view and fought for further concessions.

The system of delegations of sixty members from each of the representative bodies in Vienna and Budapest served in the place of a common parliament. Their chief duties were to control the common administration and agree on annual appropriations. The system on the whole favoured Hungary, because her delegation presented a united front and voted together, whereas the Austrians found the achievement of such unity impossible. The joint ministers often relied on the support of the Hungarian delegation, its influence being thereby increased.

An advantageous union

The economic relations between the two states were regulated by a settlement of 1868 which joined them into a customs union. Austria-Hungary earned the title *Monarchie auf Kündigung,* a state on a leasehold, since the agreement was renewable every ten years. Nevertheless, the union was based on mutual advantage: Austria was an industrial, Hungary an agricultural state. In addition, the operations of the National Austro-Hungarian Bank, guaranteed credit, detailed knowledge of the market and its peculiarities, the ties of taste and habit bound the economies of the two parts of the monarchy closely together. Between 1884 and 1891, for instance, 83–4 per cent of Hungarian imports came from Austria, while Austria took 71–5 per cent of Hungarian

exports. After that, the disparity disappeared, and by November 1906 Hungary exported nearly £40,000,000 worth of agricultural produce to Austria yearly, while Austria's exports of manufactured goods to Hungary came to much the same figure.

Separation of the two economies would have meant even more of a catastrophe for Hungary than for Austria. In their joint undertakings, Austria carried the larger share of the financial burden. Friction arose because of external rather than internal trade. A new compromise was reached in 1907: Hungary gained recognition of her right to economic independence and a long step towards commercial separation was taken. The customs union was replaced by a treaty, a court of arbitration was set up and, after 1907, foreign commercial treaties were to be made in the names of the two countries and not jointly in the name of the Emperor.

In their sharp disputes with Vienna on economic matters the Hungarians in no way acted against the spirit of the compromise of 1867. One of its chief weaknesses was the declaration of the principle of economic independence of the two parts of the Empire. Nevertheless, under the turbulent political surface, internal trade usually flowed quite smoothly. After 1867 the political structures of the two parts became more and more divergent. Roughly speaking, Vienna came to run a federation of eight nations, while the Magyars were busy constructing a national state in their own part of the monarchy.

By the turn of the century the industries of lower Austria and Bohemia had reached a stage of development similar to that in other highly industrialised countries, like England or Germany. In the decade before the outbreak of the First World War, Austrian coal production increased at a rate bettered only in Germany. In the production of pig iron Austria stood sixth in the world in 1914, its output having increased fourfold since 1890 at twice the French and sixteen times the British rate. In the same period, Austrian production of steel increased five times, and the machine tool industry about thirty times. In the last year before the outbreak of the war, the growth of production in every branch of industry was higher than the average figure for the five preceding years. The building of railways expanded rapidly so that in 1912 there were over 30,000 miles of track in the Austrian part of the monarchy alone. Though the economy of the Habsburg Empire was almost self-contained, its foreign trade increased more than five times in the years between 1863 and 1912.

Left: Advertising products of Austria's growing industry — a gramophone, and an adding and subtracting machine

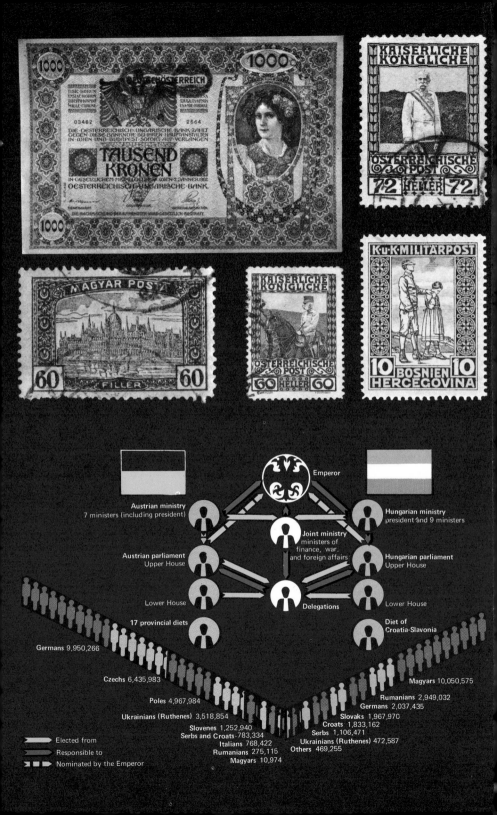

Emperor

Austrian ministry
7 ministers (including president)

Hungarian ministry
president and 9 ministers

Joint ministry
ministers of
finance, war,
and foreign affairs

Austrian parliament
Upper House

Hungarian parliament
Upper House

Lower House

Delegations

Lower House

17 provincial diets

Diet of
Croatia-Slavonia

Germans 9,950,266

Czechs 6,435,983

Poles 4,967,984

Ukrainians (Ruthenes) 3,518,854

Slovenes 1,252,940
Serbs and Croats 783,334
Italians 768,422
Rumanians 275,115
Magyars 10,974

Magyars 10,050,575

Rumanians 2,949,032
Germans 2,037,435
Slovaks 1,967,970
Croats 1,833,162
Serbs 1,106,471
Ukrainians (Ruthenes) 472,587
Others 469,255

Elected from

Responsible to

Nominated by the Emperor

Industry had more outlets and was more diversified in Bohemia and Moravia than in lower Austria. It was especially strong in its machine tool, armaments, and textile branches, and was organised in powerful cartels such as the Union of Industrialists in North Bohemia *(Verband Nordböhmischen Industrieller)* which embraced 162 firms and some 45,000 workers. In 1900 there were several districts in Bohemia where less than 10 per cent of the population was in agriculture; the movement of population into the coalfields equalled that in the Ruhr or in Belgium. Industrial and urban growth was especially fast in western and northern Bohemia, and in north-eastern Moravia.

The population of Bohemia grew from 5,000,000 to 6,500,000 in the four decades before the First World War. In 1851 there were five towns in the province with over 10,000 inhabitants; half a century later, there were forty-three. The growth and the movement of population had a far-reaching effect on the cultural structure of the Czech lands. Early in the 19th century, the Germans and the Czechs lived side by side in sharply-defined and separate settlements. The Czechs held, with the exception of the towns, the central districts; the Germans surrounded them in an arc running through the border territories of Bohemia and Moravia. That situation changed with the growth of the local industries, which made no national discrimination in its demand for labour: it was calculated that, in 1900, Czech labour was three times as mobile as German. In the Czech central districts, the urban population became mainly Czech, and the balance started changing even in the German border areas.

The Czechs accomplished their national revival under the leadership of their middle class and under the supervision of the Habsburg dynasty. František Palacký, who reconstructed their history and became the first Czech member of the Upper House in 1861, remarked that had the Habsburg Empire not existed it would have had to be invented. Another Czech leader, commenting on the ambitions of the Hungarians, said that, 'We want to create an Austria where all peoples and all provinces would be equal, not an Austria divided into two halves.' They opposed the Austro-Hungarian compromise and learned their lesson. In the last three decades of the 19th century, they fought the Austrian governments hard, and achieved some important objectives.

Above: Different stamps issued within the Empire — Austrian **(top right and bottom centre)**, Bosnian **(bottom right)** and Hungarian **(bottom left)**. Banknotes were printed by the Austro-Hungarian state bank **(top left)**. *Below:* Diagram showing the administration and population statistics of Austria-Hungary

The German monopoly over secondary education had been broken, in the 1850s, by Count Leo Thun, the first Imperial Minister of Education. Children of the Czech peasants who had come to seek work in German towns attended their own schools, and there was a university in Prague, which, in 1882, was divided into a Czech and a German part.

At first, the Czech revival was run on a shoe-string budget. Nevertheless, the Czechs shared in the growth of prosperity. Their first bank had been established in 1868, and with its help they staked out their claim to financial participation in the development of industry.

The slow decline of the German influence in the Austrian part of the monarchy, and the fast rise of the Czechs to prominence in Bohemia and Moravia increased the bitterness of politics within the Empire. Extremist parties like the German National Movement *(Deutschnationale Bewegung)* led by Georg von Schönerer in Vienna demanded that the Germans should be given a majority position in parliament. They wanted Hungary to be linked with Austria only by a personal union, and the alliance with Germany to be strengthened.

Schönerer was a violent man – he quarrelled with everyone, including his own party, and was imprisoned for an assault on one of his many political enemies. A moderate faction separated from the movement; its leaders recognised that, in alliance with Germany, the supra-national character of the monarchy could survive. Schönerer was irreconcilable. He engorged the Slavs, the Catholic Church, the Jews, the dynasty without a nationality, in a continuous, fierce battle. He became a Protestant because, in the words of his *Los-von-Rom* manifesto, 'Ever more clearly and plainly we may see the Slav insolence and Roman lust for power have closely allied themselves in the old German *Ostmark* in order to annihilate Germandom in this Empire which has been built up on German foundations.'

Young Adolf Hitler, an Austrian by birth, became an admirer of Georg von Schönerer. He hated the Habsburg State and everything it stood for, and fled to Munich in 1913 rather than serve in the Austro-Hungarian army. The situation that he experienced in Vienna before the war – the decline of the power and the influence of the Germans – occurred again, in his view, after 1918 when Germany lost the war. It was re-enacted on a large scale: instead of Austria-Hungary, the whole world witnessed

Far left: An Austrian caricature of a Magyar officer. Left from top to bottom: Julius Andrássy, the Hungarian architect of the 1867 compromise; František Palacky, Czech nationalist; Georg von Schönerer, leader of the Deutschnationale Bewegung; *Viktor Adler, leader of the Austrian Social Democrat movement*

37

the humiliation of the Germans. Hitler at once recognised the situation for what it was, and reacted in a way Schönerer would have approved of.

This was the extreme, but other parties such as the *Deutsche Arbeiterpartei* (German Workers' Party) and the Czech National Socialist Party — founded, in 1898, to combat the influence of the Marxist Social Democrats on the workers — reflected the tensions which developed in the industrial areas, where exploited workers found that the fight for existence became tangled up with the struggle for language rights, for posts in the civil service, for schools, and for the many other national properties. The first riot of German workers against Czech immigrants took place in Dessendorf in Bohemia, in 1868. In the 1880s clashes between Czech and German miners in the Bohemian coalfields involved the throwing of homemade bombs.

These parties were unable to claim a significant share of the electorate. They were fringe organisations with a limited appeal, catering for the prejudices of hardpressed workers in nationally mixed areas rather than for their basic needs and social welfare. The Social Democrats, on the other hand, had built up a mass party before the introduction of universal suffrage in the Austrian part of the monarchy in 1906. It grew out of the 'brotherhoods' *(Gesellschaften)* of journeymen and apprentices of an earlier era and the various workers' benevolent societies. Under the dedicated leadership of Viktor Adler, the Austrian Social Democrat movement won a decisive position for itself in the politics of the Empire.

Viktor Adler was born in Prague in 1852, of a wealthy Jewish family. He became politically active when he studied medicine; as a doctor he came into contact with the poor and was moved by what he saw. A few months after Marx's death, Adler came to England in the summer of 1883 to study social legislation, and formed a firm friendship with Friedrich Engels. He had a warm, compassionate personality and was liked and admired in the socialist movement.

In 1886 he used the money he inherited to found the weekly *Gleichheit,* which became the *Arbeiterzeitung,* the party newspaper, and which he edited until his death in 1918. A year before the first copy appeared, the Austrian Social Democrat Party had been formally organised at Hainfeld in December 1888. Its programme condemned national and linguistic inequality, and rejected violence as a means of advancing the socialist cause. It

Right: Karl Lueger, the Christian Socialist leader (right). **Far right:** *Austrian anti-Semitic cartoons — hated Jews flock to Palestine* **(top)***; Jew seen in the 'mirror of truth'* **(bottom)**

demanded complete political democracy, protection of civil rights, far-reaching social legislation, and free state education, and proposed to make use of the existing political institutions 'without being deceived into thinking that parliaments were other than a form of class rule'.

In 1897, the Social Democrat Party won fourteen seats in the *Reichsrat*. Ten years later, in the first elections after the introduction of universal suffrage, the number of its deputies went up to eighty-six. At the same time trade unions became an important part of the Austrian socialist movement, with 323,000 members by 1905.

The Brno programme of 1899 declared that Austria-Hungary should become a federal state of autonomous peoples: the socialist plans for the reorganisation, on national lines, of the Empire were always sensible beyond reproach. Nevertheless, national tensions had for some time made themselves felt in the party itself: Marx and Engels for instance had regarded the Slavs as being politically out of step with the rest of Europe, and some of their disciples found it difficult, despite their good intentions, to give up the habit of looking down on their Slav comrades.

Czech and German rivalry

The conflict between the Czechs and the Germans was strong enough to crack the internationalist doctrine of the party and the trade unions. The Czech Social Democrat Party had been founded in 1878 and maintained an autonomous position in the socialist movement: it sent its own delegates, for instance, to the congress of the Second International. In the last decade of the 19th century national conflict developed in the trade unions, when their membership in the Czech lands divided on national lines. Accusations of attempts to centralise and of factionalism, of German arrogance or Czech ignorance were freely exchanged. Unable to agree on the simplest issues, the two peoples started running separate trade unions.

Nevertheless, the divisions in the working-class movement were fewer than those among the middle-class parties. The Austrian middle classes had little cohesion. Their members were neither proletarian nor noble, but merged, at the upper end, with the nobility, and with the working class in the lower reaches. In Hungary the middle class consisted largely of people who were socially on the decline, while among the Czechs the middle class was composed of people who were moving in the opposite direction. The industrial and commercial bourgeoisie everywhere in the monarchy depended on the State to a large extent for the many economic concessions. It was

Left: *Czech Prague — a view taken across the River Moldau*

therefore likely to make a common cause with the State against the claims advanced by the working class. After 1879, the old Liberal Party in Austria lost much of its former following because it was not nationalist enough for some of its supporters such as Schönerer, or socialist enough for young men like Viktor Adler.

The Christian Socialists, led by Karl Lueger, also came into the inheritance left behind by Austrian liberalism. It was said of the party, which was formally constituted in 1891, that its 'history did not begin with a programme, or a manifesto, or with the resolution of a few dissenters or reformers, but with one man, Dr Karl Lueger'. Born into a lower middle-class Viennese family in 1844, Lueger remained true to his origins throughout his political career. He studied law and became a member of the City Council in 1875; he abandoned his alliance with Schönerer because Schönerer directed his appeal at middle and upper class audiences.

Though Lueger gave support to the Catholic reform movement, to the ideas on which central European Christian Socialism was based, a certain flexibility remained. Lueger became Mayor of Vienna on his fifth attempt in 1897, after opposition from the establishment, the Court, the high nobility and the clergy. He made his peace with the Court and nobility, gave firm support to the Habsburg State and, in alliance with the various clerical groups, extended his party organisation into the countryside. Lueger's Christian Socialism came to represent the revolt of the suburbs against the centre of the town. The 'little men' from the suburbs of Vienna, where the dividing line between the middle and working classes was imperceptible, gave him their unquestioning support.

The old patrician families who used to have the running of the affairs of the city in their hands did not fully grasp the implications of the growth of Vienna. In the two decades between 1870 and 1890 the population of the municipality increased threefold, some of the worst slums in Europe appeared, public services kept on breaking down. In his appeals to the Viennese Lueger linked an assault on the patrician positions with anti-Semitism. The percentage of Jews in Vienna had increased from 1.3 per cent of total population in 1857 to 12 per cent in 1890; in Budapest in 1910 the Jews accounted for almost a quarter of the inhabitants. They were attracted to certain professions: finance, medicine, law, journalism, and university teaching, all mainly city-centre pursuits. They were the leaders of the cultural life of Vienna before 1914: they wrote the most popular plays, acted in them, provided the audiences.

Lueger used the anti-Semitic platform because he knew

that it had an appeal to his voters. He had personal friends among the Vienna Jews and maintained that 'I decide who is a Jew'. Lueger told one of his Jewish friends, 'I dislike the Hungarian Jews more than I do the Hungarians, but I am no enemy of our Viennese Jews; they are not so bad and we cannot do without them.' Lueger linked corruption in political affairs with the Jews, as often as it was even remotely possible, and exploited the revulsion against urban life in all its aspects — financial, legal, and intellectual. He led the reaction against 19th-century liberalism by the people who did not understand it and who saw no way in which they benefited by it.

It was nevertheless difficult, even for sophisticated observers at the time, to see the Jewish question as part of a complex social and political development. Attempts at deeper psychological explanations could go wrong. The Jews were blamed for being rich and poor, clever and stupid; for trying to become like the rest of the population or for remaining different from it. There were some parts of the monarchy where the local population was so economically backward that it failed to develop its own middle class, and the Jews filled its place; in Slav territories anti-Semitism often became reinforced by nationalism, because the local Jews tended to identify themselves with one or the other of the leading peoples in the monarchy, and speak German or Hungarian. At the turn of the century political anti-Semitism existed wherever the Jews and the Gentiles came into contact.

When universal suffrage for males of over twenty-four years was introduced into Austria in 1906, the main divisions that followed on the break-up of Austrian liberalism had been laid down. Nevertheless, the innovation did not do away with national tensions and concentrate political interest on social problems, as its supporters had hoped. Though the system accommodated national tensions it also relied on them for its functioning; in addition, the Czech-German split inside the socialist movement had gone too far. In Hungary, instead of universal suffrage, the Agricultural Labourers Act was passed in 1907. It was meant to be a direct blow against universal suffrage; it was intended to check the flow of emigration from Hungary to the United States, and tie down the agricultural labourer more securely to his landlord and to the land he cultivated. In 1907, the first elections after the introduction of universal suffrage took place in Austria, underscoring the extent to which the two halves of the Empire had moved apart in the conduct of politics.

Left: The Czechs acclaim their Emperor in festivities at Brno

Chapter 3
Tensions within the Empire

In the last years before the war Austria-Hungary was still one of the great powers. It had a navy, but still showed no interest in acquiring colonies. Its backward agricultural territories and developed industrial areas were economically complementary but politically increasingly at odds. Yet there was no apparent reason why Austria-Hungary should not survive. Since 1870 the European powers had managed to live in peace; naturally there were differences, most of them involving the colonies. Austria was not competing in this area, but in any case such differences were always settled peaceably. The great powers also succeeded in keeping a balance in their internal politics. After the failure of the Paris Commune in 1870 the more perceptive of the revolutionaries, Friedrich Engels among them, observed with apprehension the growth of physical power at the disposal of states. Their fears were confirmed when the Tsar succeeded in crushing the revolutionaries in 1905.

In Austria, the introduction of universal suffrage did away with any hopes the Germans may have had for achieving majority in the *Reichsrat*. Their tribulations inside the monarchy were partly compensated by Austro-Hungarian foreign policy. The alliance with Germany held out to the Austrian Germans the promise that their luck might turn. It was concluded in 1879, with Italy acceding to the treaty in 1882 and Rumania two years later. The oldest dynasty in Europe found itself allied with the two youngest great powers. Both the men chiefly responsible for the treaty in 1879 — Prince Otto Bismarck and Count Julius Andrássy — had been bitter enemies of the Habsburgs. Bismarck had not rested until he made the Habsburgs snuff out their interest in the affairs of the German states. When he succeeded, however, he let the Austrians get away with the comparatively mild peace of Prague. Count Andrássy had fought in the uprising in 1848-9, and was sent as a diplomatic

Left: 1908 — the Habsburg Emperor confiscates Bosnia Herzegovina from the Turkish Empire, Franz Ferdinand declares Bulgaria's independence, and Sultan Abdul Hamid looks on sourly

45

agent of the revolutionary Hungarian government to Constantinople. After Habsburg troops, aided by the Russians, had suppressed the rising, Andrássy was tried in his absence and sentenced to death. Amnestied in 1857, he became a deputy in the Hungarian parliament in 1861 and, together with Deák, worked out the compromise of 1867. He became Foreign Minister in 1871 — his grand diplomatic strategy was to buttress the policy of compromise with an alliance between Austria, Germany, and Britain, but only a part of this plan succeeded. In 1872, together with Gorchakov and Bismarck, he formed the *Dreikaiserbund,* an alliance which gave Bismarck the opportunity of insuring against France's revenge after the Franco-Prussian War of 1870. Britain, it will be seen, was not included — Bismarck was suspicious of countries where foreign policy was under parliamentary control, as he thought it would not be stable enough. In any case, an alliance with Russia could be had more easily than Britain's friendship. However, the *Dreikaiserbund* did not last: in 1878 the Congress of Berlin failed to dispel the rivalry which developed between Austria and Russia in the Balkans after the Bosnian crisis in the summer of 1875.

The Congress of Berlin had acknowledged Rumania, Montenegro, and Serbia as independent states. Under the Obrenović kings — Milan and his son Alexander — Belgrade maintained friendly relations with Vienna. As far as the Austrians were concerned, Serbia was a small, rather poor, and rather corrupt state on the Empire's southern frontier. But there were signs of unrest in Belgrade by the turn of the century. Young Serbian politicians and officers felt that Serbia would remain economically and politically dependent on Austria-Hungary unless she could gain access to the Adriatic. Bosnia Herzegovina, occupied by Austria-Hungary, stood in the way and Russian support for Serbian ambitions was therefore essential.

In 1903 a conspiracy of these forces assassinated the King and Queen. An Obrenović was replaced by a Karageorgević, King Peter, and the assassins took positions of power — the military group under Dragutin Dimitrijević and the politicians under Nikola Pašić. A new foreign policy was initiated which relied on the backing of Russia and tried to organise the South Slavs in Austria-Hungary into an anti-Habsburg movement.

However, in 1908 an event took place which roused Serbia to more drastic policies — Austria-Hungary's Foreign Minister Aehrenthal announced that Bosnia

Left: *The three members of the* Dreikaiserbund — *Franz Joseph, Wilhelm I, Kaiser of Germany, and Tsar Alexander II of Russia*

Herzegovina was to be annexed totally into the Austro-Hungarian Empire. Whereas it had previously been administered by the Minister of Finance it was now to receive a constitution and diet of its own.

Aehrenthal had long been ambitious for Austria-Hungary to play a more assertive role in foreign affairs, and he was under the impression that he had the agreement of the Russian Foreign Minister to his action. He believed that the difference between the province before and after the annexation was largely a matter of words.

He was mistaken. The annexation of Bosnia Herzegovina brought about one of the severest international crises before the outbreak of the war. Pašić, the Serbian Foreign Minister, travelled to St Petersburg to enquire whether Russia was prepared to back Serbia in a war on Austria-Hungary. The answer was negative: on 2nd November 1908 Pašić telegraphed Belgrade from St Petersburg: 'Russia cannot and will not go to war on account of Bosnia at the present time.' Finally in March 1909 Russia, together with the other European powers, recognised the annexation of Bosnia Herzegovina. Pašić and the Serbian army had to follow the great powers' lead and calm down for the time being.

The issue was kept alive in Belgrade by other means. Shortly after the annexation, in the autumn of 1908, the Serbs founded a society called the National Defence (Narodna Obrana) which proposed to train its members in the techniques of guerilla warfare. The original intention had to be toned down when Belgrade recognised the annexation of Bosnia: the society then switched over to political and cultural agitation. It did not become any less anti-Austrian. In all of its publications it was stated that the Serbs would have no difficulty in defending themselves against Turkey's declining power and that their main effort must be aimed 'against the new Turks, who come from the north and who are more powerful and terrible than the old enemy'. The society was run by prominent members of Pašić's Radical Party as well as of the military group, and it extended its activities across the frontier to Bosnia Herzegovina and to Croatia, under the cover of a variety of gymnastic, anti-alcoholic, or literary societies.

The increase in agitation for a Greater Serbia after the Bosnian crisis alarmed the Austrian and Hungarian authorities. The two notorious political trials of the South Slavs both took place in 1909. In Croatia the Zagreb trial involving fifty-three Serbs opened in

Right: *The Congress of Berlin (1878) failed to resolve the Bosnia crisis of 1875. Bismarck shakes hands with Holstein, a German diplomat, while Austria's delegate, Andrássy, looks on*

January: they had all been arrested on charges of agitation on Serbia's behalf. Wekerle, the Hungarian Premier, accused them of high treason: the trial dragged on for several months. Though the evidence was forged, the principal defendants received sentences of up to eight years. They could not be enforced. The scandal in Croatia was matched in Austria. Heinrich Friedjung, Professor of History at Vienna University, received from Aehrenthal in March 1909 some documents containing details of subversion by Serbia and implicating South Slav politicians in Austria-Hungary. Friedjung wrote an article on the basis of the documents, which was published in the *Neue Freie Presse* on 25th March 1909. It stated that, 'If the Austrian army were given the job of cleaning up the Belgrade nest of revolutionaries it would perform a civilising mission of the highest order.' Members of the Serbo-Croat Coalition, the leading political party in Croatia, were accused of receiving money and of acting in collusion with the Serbian government. The members of the coalition sued Friedjung for libel: the historian was unable to prise out of Aehrenthal the originals of the documents he had seen the copies of. Worse still, the trial showed that they had been forged.

The two attempts to show the duplicity, and perhaps treason, in a court of law resulted in a sharp decline in the credibility of the Vienna government. The trials were hastily prepared, had to rely on forged evidence, and showed the unreasoning hostility of the Austro-Hungarian authorities to the South Slavs. It did not mean that all the accusations were ludicrous. The intentions of the Belgrade government towards Vienna were no less hostile than the other way round.

In the meanwhile, contacts between Belgrade and the South Slavs of the Habsburg Empire increased. Serbian schools and universities were thrown wide open to students from Austria-Hungary. Neither the Serbian army nor the civil service made any distinction between native-born Serbs and those who were technically Habsburg subjects. Serbia supplied schools and universities in Austria-Hungary with periodicals and other propaganda material, in some cases even with text-books.

One of the worst difficulties of the situation was that any adoption of a conciliatory attitude to the South Slavs, on the part of the Imperial authorities, was often worse than useless: a population happily occupied with its local pursuits was the last thing the politicians and soldiers in Belgrade wanted. In 1910, the first Diet opened in

Top left: Sarajevo is taken by Austrian troops, 1878. **Bottom left:** *The nightmare of the Habsburgs — Germany, Italy, and Russian reach out to take their share of the Empire's territories*

Bosnia. The province was expected to develop some degree of self-government. Four months later, Bogdan Zerajić, a young Serb student, fired at the Governor. He missed and shot himself instead. After his death he was described by the Belgrade press as a martyr for the Serbian cause. A friend of his wrote a poem about Zerajić, which fired the imagination of his contemporaries on both sides of the frontier.

The attempt on the life of the Governor of Austria marked a watershed in the assault, by Belgrade, on the Habsburg Balkan strongholds. The stress shifted again, from political and cultural agitation to direct terrorist action. In May 1911, the terrorist group was given a new, more menacing name. It was called Unity or Death *(Ujedinjenje ili Smrt)* and become known as the 'Black Hand'. It was under the control of the group of military conspirators who had organised the assassination of the king and queen in 1903. The 'special duty officers' on the Austrian and Turkish frontiers, appointed by the General Staff, were usually members of the Black Hand Society. It regarded assassinations and acts of terror in the 'not yet liberated territories' as necessary in the interests of the Serbian people. It was responsible for many of them.

But soon the surface peace in the Balkans was disturbed by a new series of wars. Turkey in Europe still embraced Albania, Macedonia, Thessaly, and Thrace before the Balkan Wars. Its hold on these populations, however, was precarious; always on the brink of revolution, the subject peoples rose again in 1912. The first Balkan War was an attack on these remaining positions of Turkey in Europe by Montenegro, Bulgaria, Serbia, and Greece; in the second war, Bulgarian gains were chiefly disputed by her former allies. After a campaign begun in October of 1912, Turkey collapsed at the end of the year. Hostilities flared up again in January 1913, when the Turks attempted to prevent the surrender of Adrianople. It fell on 26th March. The territorial settlement achieved at the Conference of London, however, created new differences in the Balkans, and the alliances rearranged themselves in time for the second Balkan War. In order to divide Macedonia in their own way, the Serbs and the Greeks formed an alliance; the Bulgarians attacked them on 28th June 1913, and were, in their turn, attacked by the Rumanians a fortnight later. A day later, on 12th July, the Turks began to advance into Thrace, recapturing Adrianople from the Bulgarians on the way. The peace of Bucharest in August 1913 gave Serbia a large part of Macedonia including the towns of Skopje and Monastir. An Austrian ultimatum to Belgrade in October 1913,

Left: A Serbian anti-Austria protest meeting in Belgrade

53

however, forced the Serbs to withdraw from the border territory in Albania. The territorial settlement after the Balkan Wars was so complex that it could not be completed in time for the outbreak of the First World War.

But the Balkans were not the only place where peace between Russia and the Habsburg Empire was disturbed. Hartwig, the Russian Minister to Belgrade, supported, as much as he could, the Great Serbian aspirations before the outbreak of the war. In the Balkans, Russia's support for an anti-Habsburg movement was official and indirect: in eastern Galicia, another highly sensitive area, it was unofficial and direct. In eastern Galicia, where the landlords were, as a rule, Poles while the peasants were Ruthene, two political trends had developed in the decades before the outbreak of the war. The Old Ruthene Party tended to regard the people as a part, historically as well as linguistically, of the Russian nation; the Ukrainian Party, on the other hand, argued that the differences between the Ukrainians (or Ruthenes) and the Russians were so great that they and the Russians were two quite separate peoples. In the years before the war, the Ukrainian Party got the upper hand. After the elections to the *Reichsrat* of 1911, it sent twenty-one deputies to Vienna and the Old Ruthenes only two.

Whatever their party allegiance, the Ukrainians had received support from Vienna. There were signs that the government welcomed the emergence of another nationality which could, if needed, be used to offset the claims advanced on behalf of the Poles. In the years before the war the Ukrainians were making a claim to have their own university at Lemberg and it appeared that the Emperor was favourably disposed towards it. Nevertheless, the decline in its political fortunes as well as the increase of international tension after the Bosnian crisis, pushed the Old Ruthene Party into opposition and then, into revolt against Habsburg rule.

Panslav unrest
The anti-Habsburg movement was supported by the Slav nationalist societies in Russia, and aided by the peculiar religious situation in the province, as well as by the political simplicity of the Ruthene peasants. Like the Pan-German movement in Berlin, Panslavism in St Petersburg did not exercise much influence on official foreign policy before the war. A few newspapers and a lot of retired generals gave it their support. Its public expressions – societies, exhibitions, congresses – were inspired by comradely feelings of racial, or linguistic, or religious affinities rather than by hard political calculation. The Orthodox Church helped by converting the Ruthene peasants from Greek Catholicism to Greek

Orthodoxy. (The Greek Catholic, or Uniate, Church recognised the Roman ecclesiastical hierarchy but used Orthodox rites.) The prayer books were manufactured at a monastery near Kiev and smuggled into eastern Galicia. In that way some Ruthene peasants, subjects of Franz Joseph I, suddenly found themselves praying for the Tsar and the Russian army.

The Galician-Russian society, run by a Duma deputy called Count Bobrinski, was also becoming more active in the years before the war. On 30th November 1913, for instance, it organised a large meeting in St Petersburg, the main purpose of which was to describe the desperate situation in the province after the failure of the harvest. Count Bobrinski was in the chair; Demetrius Markov, one of the two Ruthene deputies to the *Reichsrat,* was a guest of honour, together with an imported Ruthene peasant, who sat on the platform and did not say much. Bobrinski told the audience that 110,000,000 Russians should be able to help their 4,000,000 brothers on the other side of the frontier and presented Markov with a wreath with the inscription: 'To the brave fighter for the Russian language.'

The pro-Russian agitation flowed over into other Ruthene provinces, in Bukovina and Carpathian Russia, in north-eastern Hungary. In the winter of 1913-14, pamphlets were circulated in Carpathian Russia attacking the Uniate Church and accusing the Budapest government of inhuman oppression of the Ruthene people: 'Every Russian, even if he is not a subject of the Tsar, everyone in whom flows a drop of Slav blood has the duty to pray for Him and His Family, because He is the only protector the Slavs have on this earth. The fame of great Russia is infinite: she is a sister of the Russians in Hungary . . . Fear not, the Russian nation is great and powerful and on our side. We shall be victorious.'

The Austro-Hungarian authorities were as much concerned with the growth of pro-Russian agitation in the north of the monarchy as with the Serbian propaganda in the Balkans. On 19th January 1914, the Governor of Galicia reported to the Ministry of the Interior that '. . . recently, the agitation of the Russophil party . . . has become more lively: it is partly concerned with strengthening its political organisation and partly with the education of the younger generation in its own spirit . . . The schismatic propaganda is also gaining in strength; new Orthodox emissaries have appeared in the district . . . The continuing Russification of Galicia, aided by Orthodoxy, requires greater attention on the part of the administrative officers if they are to be able to combat it . . .'

Left: *Serbian troops are mobilised during the Bosnian crisis*

The Governor of Galicia asked the civil servants to watch over the activities of the pro-Russian societies. The new Ukrainian organisations were usually successful in countering political propaganda, but they found it more difficult to combat religious offshoots. In parishes looked after by pro-Russian priests, Greek Orthodoxy became firmly entrenched: an uneasy situation on a very sensitive frontier.

As in the Balkans, the Hungarian authorities took the initiative first: in February 1914 a trial of the Ruthenes opened at Marmaros-Sziget. Count Bobrinski himself came to Marmaros as a witness. On 3rd March 1914, thirty-two Ruthenes received short sentences, the severest one being four and a half years' imprisonment and a small fine—passed on the parish priest. A week later, a similar trial opened in the east Galician capital, Lemberg. After long, meandering proceedings the jury declared the four defendants not guilty on charges of treason and espionage.

Though pro-Russian opinions were not in themselves illegal, and though the prosecution found it impossible to produce convincing evidence of espionage, the civil authorities went on keeping a close watch on the pro-Russian movement. The movement itself was disturbingly elusive, and its ramifications reached not only into Russia, but into other Slav lands of the Habsburg Empire. The famine relief fund, for instance, collected by Bobrinski's society, was passed on to Galicia by a Prague bank run by pro-Russian Czechs.

The movement in east Galicia did not escape the notice of the Foreign Ministry. In a way it was more dangerous than the anti-Habsburg activities of the Serbs because Russia herself was directly involved. Leopold Count Berchtold was the Minister of Foreign Affairs: he had replaced Aehrenthal in 1912. Though Berchtold had the Friedjung trial to learn from, he did little to stop the two Ruthene trials from going ahead. He had spent an important part of his diplomatic career in St Petersburg but he failed to keep in touch with the Russians on matters concerning the two countries as often as Aehrenthal had done. He was an aristocrat who was dedicated to the dynasty and always looked forward to his audiences with the Emperor; nevertheless, he had less intelligence, and far less ambition, than his predecessor. In April 1914

Top: *King Peter I of Serbia, the Karageorgevic usurper, his sceptre bearing the heads of his assassinated Obrenovic predecessors, King Alexander and Queen Draga (**left**). Turkey, satirised as the 'Fat Ma' of Europe, watches tearfully as Austria strips her of Bosnia and Herzegovina in 1908 (**right**). **Bottom:** Franz Joseph visits the Bosnian capital, Sarajevo, in 1910*

57

he suggested to the Minister of the Interior that it should run three separate surveys, dealing with pro-Russian agitators, newspapers, and societies. The minister thought it was a good idea but did nothing about it before the outbreak of the war.

Berchtold regarded the Ruthene movement as the most important of the national questions which affected foreign policy because of its repercussions on the relations between Austria and Russia. 'It is no exaggeration,' he wrote to Stürgkh, the Austrian premier, 'when I say that our relations with Russia, which are of such great importance, will depend in the future on our success in preventing the Russification of the Ruthenes, which is being vigorously pursued on our territory, and in preserving the separate character of this nation, and by raising its civilisation.'

Berchtold wrote this note early in June 1914. At the end of the month, Franz Ferdinand and his wife were assassinated in Sarajevo. The Minister of War, General Krobatin, as well as the Hungarian Premier, Count Tisza, were also concerned about the growing seriousness of the Ruthene problem. They later made the decision to go to war with Serbia against the background of the growing tension with Russia.

Firm and able leadership

The Bosnian crisis, the Balkan Wars, and the international disturbances connected with them, were reflected in Czech politics as well. Their major political parties – the Agrarians and the Social Democrats – presented on the whole a stolid, unshaken front. The Agrarian Party was under a firm and able leadership, conscious of its power and responsibility to both the Empire and the Czech people. Its leaders went on playing the Habsburg political game by its usual rules. So did the Social Democrats, who believed, as all Marxists do, in large economic units (i.e. the Empire rather than small, independent states) and who tended to put the solution of the national after that of the social problem. The two smaller clerical parties in Bohemia and Moravia were also entirely loyal to the monarchy, regarding it as the embodiment of all political virtues.

The Czechs who ran those parties, although sometimes resentful of its remoteness, were impressed by the Court in Vienna. They may have opposed the government, but never the existence of the state itself. Among the smaller, more nationally-minded parties, however, there were some signs of opposition to the Habsburg Empire. The small Progressive Party, which sent two deputies to the *Reichsrat,* took an open stand against the Habsburg State before the war, but was the only Czech political party to

do so.

The German alliance, as we have seen, reconciled some of the Austrian-German politicians to the situation in Austria-Hungary and antagonised some of their Slav colleagues. Though the Panslavism of the Czechs was closely linked with their national revival, their contacts with Russia in the 19th century remained confined to cultural exchanges. They may have had political overtones, but no more. The Czechs, most of them Catholics, lacked the religious bond of the Ruthenes or the Serbs to the Russians. After the turn of the century, the situation began to change. The all-Slav congresses in Prague and St Petersburg in 1908 and in Sofia in 1910 had political rather than literary character; the plan for a Slav bank was first put forward by the Czechs in 1908. Between the end of the Balkan Wars and the outbreak of the First World War the Panslav movement acquired a sharp anti-Habsburg edge.

Karel Kramář was the chairman of the Young Czech Party, a medium-sized middle-class organisation, and a deputy to the *Reichsrat*. A forceful and opinionated man, often at loggerheads with his own party, he had married a Russian woman and, apart from political contacts, had business connections with Russia. He usually spent the summers at his magnificent house in the Crimea. Kramář believed that Slav unity was the only reliable defence against encroachments by Prussia. He made an attempt to interest the Habsburg ruler in the idea, but did not get very far and had to abandon his hopes of becoming a Habsburg Foreign Minister who would lead the Empire from the German into the Russian camp.

One of Kramář's friends was the central European representative of the St Petersburg Telegraph Agency, Svatkovski, who was in touch with the Russian Foreign Ministry. In May 1914 Kramář put his proposals down in writing. Assuming that there would be a war between Russia and Austria-Hungary, and that Austria-Hungary would break up, he proposed that it should be replaced by a Slav federation. This would resemble the Habsburg Empire in many ways although the Tsarist regime being what it was, the central authority would probably have been tighter. Kramář was unworried about that; he assumed that the Poles could somehow be coaxed into the federation, and that the Balkan countries, Serbia among them, would give up their newly won independence. On 16th June 1914 Svatkovski passed Kramář's proposal on to the Russian Ambassador to Vienna. His covering note for the Foreign Minister was terse: 'The project is of a

Left: *Shevket Pasha (right), leader of the Young Turks who threatened to reinvigorate the corpse of the Turkish Empire*

fantastic nature, and because of the serious consequences it might have for its authors, I regard it as my duty to request most humbly that it be kept in strict confidence.' For Kramář, it was a second-string plan. Before the Habsburg Empire broke up, he continued to act as a Habsburg politician and, two weeks after his proposal had been forwarded to St Petersburg, he came forward with a most forceful condemnation of the assassins of the Heir Apparent. At that time, apart from the Russians, only his two closest friends knew about the secret plan.

Having benefited by the introduction of general suffrage, the National Socialist Party had grown bigger than the Young Czechs. They were represented in the *Reichsrat* by thirteen deputies and led by Václav Klofáč. Since the turn of the century Klofáč had tried hard to wean Czech workers away from Social Democrat, Marxist influence, believing that the workers were more interested in the solution of the national rather than their immediate social problems. He was an unscrupulous politician, intensely chauvinist, and pro-Russian, and came out with an even more fantastic project than Kramář's. On 22nd January 1914 Zhukovski, the Russian Consul in Prague, telegraphed the Foreign Ministry that Klofáč and a Prague banker would arrive in the Russian capital in a few days, and that they did not want to have their visit reported in the newspapers.

Klofáč wanted to consult the Russians on the organisation, in case of war, of anti-Habsburg resistance in the Czech lands. He knew well the situation in Serbia and had in mind a network of agents on the South Slav secret organisation lines. It was to be especially strong in the eastern districts of the Czech lands; Zhukovski described Klofáč's plan as an 'attempt to facilitate Russian intelligence activities'. When Sazanov, the Russian Foreign Minister, received Klofáč on 24th January 1914, he made a reference to 'war-mongering adventurers' in Europe, men like Enver Pasha in Constantinople, or the Crown Prince in Vienna, or the King of Bulgaria. Nevertheless, Sazanov said, reports from European capitals gave him confidence in peace. Sazanov then asked the Czech politician what would happen in his country if war broke out. Klofáč's evasive reply was that the Czechs were not yet ready for a revolution.

When Klofáč saw the Chief of the Russian General Staff a few days later, he was told that although Russia did not want war, she was ready for it. Klofáč then described to him his plans for an intelligence network, and eventually agreed to discuss his suggestion with the Russian Military Attaché in Vienna. Back in Austria, Klofáč did not venture to contact the Military Attaché. He talked to his friend, the Russian Consul in Prague, instead, and

gave him a memorandum which Zhukovski passed on to the Embassy in Vienna on 25th April 1914. It argued that the interests of the Tsarist Empire and of Klofáč's National Socialist Party were identical, and asked the Russians to help the party, promising that the party would help them. It would carry pro-Russian propaganda into the eastern provinces of the Czech lands, and prepare them for the occupation by Russian armies. Klofáč even let the Russians know exactly how much it would cost to open new party HQ and run local newspapers. He added that, 'In eastern Moravia and Silesia the secret aim of the secretariats should be the building up of a network based on every town and village so that in case of a Russian advance across Silesia into eastern Moravia people should be available on whom the Russian army could completely rely.'

A dubious outlook

Neither the Young Czechs nor the National Socialists were aware of their leaders' Russian plans. Had they known of them, they probably would have disapproved. The proposals made the Russian diplomats rather nervous: the Austrian authorities, although they were concerned about the pro-Russian agitation in the Czech lands, were ignorant of Kramář's and Klofáč's secret activities. When the Austro-Hungarian government scanned the political situation in its Slav territories in the months before the war, it was not reassuring. Nevertheless, the terrorist activities in the South Slav territories, the pro-Russian propaganda in the Czech lands, and the weird blend of religious and political agitation among the Ruthenes, were to external appearances only marginal phenomena. There was hope that they would subside, that peace would in the end prevail. Anyway, the majority of Slav politicians were quite happy in the monarchy.

The Rumanians of Transylvania and the Italian minority in Austria were also generally quiescent in the last four decades before the war. After the secret treaty with Vienna and Berlin in 1883, King Carol I of Rumania discouraged every form of irredentist movement by the Rumanian subjects of Austria-Hungary: Italy was also allied with the two central Empires, and no trouble was therefore expected, or indeed coming, from the Austrian Italians. The situation changed dramatically during the war, when Italy and Rumania joined the ranks of Austria's enemies. For the time being, however, it appeared to be neither desperate nor serious. But how far this impression was true was to be shown by subsequent events.

Left: Serbian women train for the defence of their country

Chapter 4
Vienna: City of Frivolity and Achievement

Against this background of national tension and discord Vienna went on leading its customary easy-going life. The last social season before the outbreak of the First World War was as gay as the one before. Strauss's and Lanner's waltzes were as delightful as when they had first been heard; the restaurants at the Sacher and the Imperial hotels were visited as much by Viennese society as by visitors to the capital. The season ended late in February with the beginning of Lent.

Court ceremonies went on being just as impressive and beautiful as ever, closely linked with the feasts of the Church. The Viennese sense of occasion and theatrical effect displayed the many elements of pomp to their best advantage. The costumes of the nobility, some brilliant and others sombre, the lavish use on them of furs, especially silver fox and sable; the gold embroidery on dark uniforms, the exotic leopard-skin attilas, held together by big clasps of beaten silver; Knights of the Golden Fleece, archbishops, and bishops in their ancient, priceless robes, these ingredients went into the making of every court occasion, hauntingly lovely to look at, tremendously exhausting to take part in.

Even the symbolic display of humility on Maundy Thursday was in its way grand and impressive. In the Rittersaal ladies in black and men in dress uniforms, members of the Imperial House as well as of the diplomatic corps, watched the Emperor wash the feet of other old men, each of them sitting on a stool, with a Life Guard standing to attention behind every one of them. On Good Friday there followed in the Court Chapel the solemnly magnificent ceremony of the Holy Sepulchre. On fine days there was a procession, the windows of the old Burg full of faces. At 4 pm the clock in Amalienhof struck; the Knights of the Teutonic Order appeared in the Schweitzertor and came to a sudden halt; the national anthem sounded as if it came from a great distance, and then the blast of a single trumpet called everyone to

Left: The greatest Roman Catholic power in the world — the Habsburg Emperor participates in the Good Friday ceremony

63

prayer. Under the baldachin in the gateway communion was received, acolytes briskly swinging their censers. Then the *Te Deum* was sung inside the Chapel, completing the religious part of the ceremony. The military band struck up, and the troops marched past the Emperor.

The Corpus Christi procession outshone all others. The restraint of Lent and the grave pomp of Easter had been left behind: this was a dazzling occasion. The soldiers and gendarmes lining the streets had ivy leaves in their helmets; the archdukes arrived separately, in crystal calèches drawn by six greys; then the Emperor, accompanied by Archduke Franz Ferdinand, came in a carriage of gold and crystal, drawn by eight horses. But some connoisseurs of court ceremonial maintained that Habsburg funerals stood in a class of their own. When the murdered Empress Elizabeth returned to her city, on a warm September night, it was completely silent, and plunged in darkness. On the route between the Westbahn railway station and the Hofburg the darkness was relieved by torches fixed to the street lamps, faintly illuminating the faces in the crowd. The cortège moved slowly down the slope, the silence broken only by the click of the hooves against the cobble-stones.

The ceremonial occasions bound the rulers and the ruled together by invisible links, but they gave more pleasure to the ruled. The aristocracy, in the years before the war still the richest and most powerful social group in Vienna, found their pleasures elsewhere. The families with historic names had their boxes at the Imperial Theatre and at the Opera, but their interest in the arts did not go much beyond that. The aristocracy of birth and the aristocracy of intellect rarely mixed in Vienna. Women of noble birth organised occasions to amuse themselves and their men: charity balls during the season, charity concerts during Lent, the *tableaux vivants,* the uneasy blend of pantomime without words and ballet without dancing, as often as they could get enough good-looking young men and women to take part in them.

Nevertheless, the aristocrats spent only the smaller part of the year in the city. They started leaving it towards the end of March and did not return much before the end of November, unless they absolutely had to. Their lives still revolved around the country houses and the land that surrounded them: they found the pleasures of the countryside, hunting and shooting, as well as their horses, more absorbing than anything the town could provide. The size and comfort of their country houses was usually a better index of their social and financial stand-

Right: The wedding of Archduke Karl to Princess Zita. Emperor Franz Joseph is standing beside the mother of the bridegroom

ing than their town residences. Their physical as well as spiritual remoteness from the city and its pursuits, from its intellectual as well as common life, surrounded the aristocracy by an impenetrable barrier. Its more fortunate members lived out their enchanted lives before the outbreak of the First World War.

Soon after the noblemen returned to town in November, the Hofball opened the season. But the grand balls – the most successful of them were usually organised by Princess Pauline Metternich – were only a small part of the stream of Viennese entertainment. Every society, every social group had its own ball. The journalists had a very good one; so did the chimney sweeps, the guild of butchers, the circle of cyclists. Night after night, formal dancing was going on somewhere in Vienna.

Those were the red letter days in the calendars of the common people of Vienna; otherwise they led their comfortable everyday lives with as much decorum as they could either afford or bear. They were extremely fond of their food and drink – the beers and wines they drank were much lighter than their favourite dumplings, noodles, and pastries. Frivolity and charm came easily to them; there was not a trace of dourness about them. Their fondness for official titles, the longer the better, was among their few failings.

A flowering of civilisation

Robert Musil, who set his novel, *The Man Without Qualities,* in the last year of peace, described Vienna in that period by contrasting it with 'a kind of super-American city'. In that city, 'air and earth form an anthill, veined by channels of traffic' where everybody has a definite task to accomplish, before returning, in the evening, to find at home – in another tower, in another part of the town – 'Wife, family, gramophone, and soul'. Vienna, on the other hand, was 'somewhat smaller than all the rest of the world's largest cities, but nevertheless quite considerably larger than a mere ordinary large city'. And it was set in 'that misunderstood state that has since vanished', where there was speed but not too much of it; where there were cars, but not too many; where large sums were spent on the army, 'but only just enough to assure one of remaining the second weakest among the great powers'.

It was a state, in Musil's view, which had no ambition to combine the acquisition of world markets or world power with an enlightened bureaucracy. It had only 71 ▷

Left: Emperor Franz Joseph receiving Kaiser Wilhelm II and a deputation of German princes at Schönbrunn. Next page: Karl Lueger, Mayor of Vienna in 1897, rides through the Prater

one defect: it regarded genius or enterprise of genius in private citizens, 'unless privileged by high birth or State appointment, as ostentation, indeed presumption'. There was compensation for that: in the Habsburg Empire, 'a genius was always regarded as a lout, but never, as sometimes happened elsewhere, that a mere lout was regarded as a genius'. It was, in Musil's view, a home for genius: 'and that, probably, was the ruin of it'.

In the last years of peace in Vienna, following hard on the growth of the city's size, and riches, and problems, there took place an extraordinary flowering of its culture. The philosophical foundations had been laid by Ernst Mach, the scientist and philosopher, a passionate enemy and devastating critic of dogmatic statement of any kind. His influence on contemporary literature is exemplified by Robert Musil's 'man without qualities', a character constantly in the throes of contradiction: an idea is proposed, discussed, accepted—and then suddenly and completely undercut by another, equally valid, but totally contradictory proposition. Logic, the mainstay of philosophical inquiry, dissolves into absurdity as its claims and pretensions are, one by one, shown to lack substance.

Whereas Ernst Mach was concerned with a critique of reason as a scientific or philosophical instrument, Sigmund Freud set out to analyse the motive forces of human behaviour. He had published his first contribution to normal psychology, *The Interpretation of Dreams (Die Traumdeutung),* in 1900. He was then working in isolation, on what he regarded as the main task of his life: 'To infer or to guess how the mental apparatus is constructed and what forces interplay and counteract in it.' His work slowly gained recognition among his colleagues, who met for the first time in 1908 at the International Congress of Psychoanalysis. Freud, like Mach, had widespread influence on the literature of the time. His psychoanalytic methods were exploited by Arthur Schnitzler, a doctor by training, whose sad comedies of seduction became vehicles for dissecting the incompatibility of men and women. His best-known novel, *Der Weg ins Freie (The Way into the Open),* was published in 1908.

Karl Kraus, the waspish editor of *Die Fackel (The Torch),* specialised in a particularly virulent kind of satire. Schnitzler's work was roundly attacked by Kraus who, although himself a Jew, accused Schnitzler of writing for an audience of Jewish intellectuals suffering from fatty degeneration of the mind. Despite his often rather unpleasantly arrogant disposition, Kraus 74 ▷

Left: The splendour and gaiety of the Viennese season. Franz Joseph makes an appearance at one of the many gala events

'A home for genius'

While Vienna's aristocracy danced the season away, the arts flourished in every field, patronised by those who very often came under fire from the *literati*, and men of genius initiated movements that were to influence the whole of European culture. Viennese artists brought their romanticism to the new impressionist paintings; Mahler took time off from the Viennese Opera to experiment with new musical ideas, though none so revolutionary as Schönberg's twelve-tone scale. Philosophical inquiry reached new heights in the keenly critical writings of Ernst Mach, and Sigmund Freud delved into the secrets of human motivation. The brittle superficiality of Viennese life was brilliantly satirised in the comedies of Arthur Schnitzler and the cogent observations of Karl Kraus, the editor of *Die Fackel*. **Top right:** A group of artists—Gustav Klimt is in the armchair. **Bottom right:** Klimt's studio, with his last painting. **Below:** Part of Freud's study in Vienna.

possessed a biting satirical wit, and commanded a large
following of admirers. Even today, the trenchancy of some
of his remarks can be enjoyed. In his campaign for a reform
of the laws relating to sexual offences, Kraus wrote:
'A trial involving sexual morality is a deliberate step
from individual to general immorality.' Freud's psychoanalysis he described as 'the disease of which it pretends
to be the cure'. He was equally outspoken on political
issues, and could, when he chose, be very perceptive.
Certainly he realised the extent of the economic and
social changes in Austria and Germany, and understood
the implications of the fact that there had been no com-
parable political change (as there had been in England
and France) to accommodate these.

In the creative arts, especially in painting, the *fin de
siècle* mood — of autumn, of leave-taking, of decline, of
brown muted colours — merged with the earlier romantic
Austrian school. It produced a steady supply of paintings
suitable for the dark and spacious Viennese flats. Gustav
Klimt continued to delight his public with the visions of
diffuse sunlight in deserted woods. But there were signs
of change. Oskar Laske, who was soon to become the
official war artist, painted in a way reminiscent of the
French impressionists. Oskar Kokoschka was a student
at the Viennese School of Arts and Crafts in the years
1905-9, developing his own style, combining strikingly
bright colours with bold, uncompromising brush strokes.

In music, too, it was a time for experiment. Gustav
Mahler, the son of a poor Jew from a village in Bohemia,
reigned over the Viennese Opera in the decade up to the
year 1907. The perfectionist standards — which he im-
posed on all who worked with him — eventually made him
very unpopular and this, combined with the habitual
Viennese anti-Semitism, forced his resignation, an event
which Mahler himself only survived for four years. As a
composer, Mahler experimented with many means of
musical expression; he introduced various elements, including folk music, into his compositions so that they
sometimes resembled a collage painting. His *Lieder*
(songs) broke the traditional rules, often sounding like
notes for symphonies: Mahler in the end fused the two
forms in *Das Lied von der Erde*, part *Lied*, part symphony.
Arnold Schönberg experimented in a different way, with
the conventional tonal system until, soon after the First
World War, he designed the twelve-tone system of his

Far right: Poster by Kokoschka for an art exhibition in Vienna.
*Right: Arnold Schönberg **(top)** and Gustav Mahler **(upper
centre)**, fathers of modern music; Ernst Mach, the physicist
and philosopher **(lower centre)**; Robert Musil **(bottom)** a
novelist who was greatly influenced by the work of Mach*

own. Mahler and Schönberg were undoubtedly the founders of the modern movement in music.

As long as peace and the rule of law were maintained, the many components that made up the rich diversity of the Empire and its capital lived side by side. There was conflict and friction among them, but at no time did the various forces combine against the State. Slav dissent, we have seen, was marginal, but proved to be the writing on the wall. As 1914 approached, it was to be seen more and more clearly in Bosnia Herzegovina, the last acquisition of Franz Joseph's reign.

Apart from the largely peaceful population, the ordinary poor people earning their living, there were two groups in Bosnia Herzegovina with totally incompatible views of its future. On the one hand, there were the civil servants, under the Minister of Finance, who were trying to solve the problem of the two provinces' backwardness and poverty. Their problems were those of industrialisation and modern administration, but on the whole these were well understood and efficiently dealt with. On the other hand, there was a small group of terrorists, most of them under twenty-one, and great idealists. They were familiar with the radical political literature of Bakunin, Kropotkin, and Marx, but despite anarchist and socialist influences, these young men became romantic nationalists. They displayed no interest in their country's economic and social advancement. Those two groups—the civil servants and young terrorists—had nothing in common and, had any of them ever met, they would have confronted each other with blank incomprehension.

Beginning of the end

The terrorists were dedicated to doing away with Austrian rule in Bosnia Herzegovina. A group of young Bosnian Serbs in Belgrade, headed by the student Gavrilo Princip, received much help from Colonel Dimitrijević and his associates. A few months before Archduke Franz Ferdinand's visit to Sarajevo, this group was trained in terrorist techniques, given arms and ammunition, and an introduction to a special duties officer who saw them safely across the Austro-Hungarian frontier. The Serbian Prime Minister did nothing to stop them. He had had sharp differences with the military on the administration of the newly acquired territories in Macedonia, and it may be that he did not want to antagonise the military any further. On 28th June they killed the Archduke and his wife at Sarajevo.

The assassinations took place in the middle of a hot

Right: Art nouveau poster advertising an Austrian calender

summer, the politicians were away from their posts, diplomatic business was conducted at a leisurely pace. It looked as if nobody wanted to be disturbed by the Sarajevo incident. In Vienna itself, when the news broke on Sunday afternoon, people were neither sad nor bent on revenge; the bands in Prater and Grinzing went on playing as if nothing had happened. There were only the special editions of newspapers, with thick black edges. On Tuesday, 30th June 1914, the Russian Ambassador reported that, 'The tragic end of Archduke Franz Ferdinand found little response here and on the stock exchange, this index of the mood in the business circles. The value of government stocks did not change, which is explained here by confidence in the continuation of peace.' The Budapest stock exchange registered an upward trend. The Archduke was even less liked in Hungary than in Austria.

There was speculation in the Viennese press on the connections between the assassin and Belgrade, while in Belgrade 'the Jewish press' of Vienna was sharply attacked. There were anti-Serb riots in Sarajevo. The opinion of the political leaders in Vienna was deeply divided. The Chief of Staff, Conrad von Hötzendorf, returned to Vienna at once, and told his friends that 'the outrage was a Serbian machination, that it had created an extremely serious situation and would lead to war with Serbia; this brought with it the danger that Russia and Rumania would have to be counted as enemies'. The Foreign Minister, Count Berchtold, was also convinced that the time had come to settle accounts with Serbia.

Stefan Tisza, the Hungarian Premier, however, was sharply opposed to war. The son of another Prime Minister, Tisza was one of the most influential men in the monarchy. He had studied in Germany when Bismarck was at the height of his power, and saw the alliance with Germany as the ultimate guarantee of Austria's security, especially in case of war. When he came to Vienna on 29th June and was told by Berchtold of his views, Tisza replied that he regarded a war on Serbia as a fatal mistake. He spent the following two days talking to Viennese politicians and drafting a memorandum for the Emperor. He argued that there was no sufficient evidence of Serbia's guilt, and that the Belgrade government might be able to provide a satisfactory explanation.

Tisza regarded this as an unsuitable time for an action on Serbia. Bulgaria had been weakened in the Balkan Wars, and Rumania all but lost. The Balkan peninsula was never at a loss for reasons for war. The Prime Minister begged the Emperor to raise the matter of Rumania and Bulgaria with Kaiser Wilhelm II, when he came to Vienna

Right: Poster announcing the Emperor's forthcoming Jubilee

for the Archduke's funeral. But Franz Joseph was coming round to the views of the war party. He knew the risks involved. He told his Chief of Staff that, 'If the monarchy is doomed to perish, let it at least perish decorously!'

The most radical and best solution

On 5th July 1914 Conrad had another audience in which he once more told the Emperor of his conviction that war on Serbia could no longer be avoided. The Emperor agreed and added, 'Are you sure of Germany?' On the same day at luncheon, the Austrian Ambassador to Berlin handed over a comprehensive memorandum on the Balkan situation to the Kaiser, together with a covering note from Franz Joseph. The Kaiser read the two documents in the Ambassador's presence and when he finished he said that he expected Austria to act against Serbia and that, because of the wider European repercussions of the action, he would have to consult his Chancellor. On the following day, the Ambassador reported that the German government recognised 'the danger presented to Austria-Hungary and the Triple Alliance by the Russian policy of alliances on the Balkans'. The Germans believed, the Ambassador continued, that Austria was the best judge of what her policy in the Balkans should be, and that she could rely on Germany as an ally and a friend whatever she decided to do. The Ambassador added that the Chancellor 'like his Imperial master, regards our immediate intervention against Serbia as the most radical and best solution of our difficulties in the Balkans'.

On 6th July, the arrival of the first telegram from Berlin brought Berchtold the news of the Ambassador's lunch with the Kaiser. Immediately he summoned Conrad, with the aim of discovering the Emperor's real intentions. He also told Conrad the news from Berlin, and the resolution to go to war, on the part of Vienna, began to grow stronger. On 7th July 1914 the council of the joint ministers met in Vienna. Stefan Tisza agreed with Berchtold that the position had changed in the past few days and that the possibility of a military intervention against Serbia was not as remote as he had thought it was immediately after the assassination. But Tisza said that he would not agree to a surprise attack on Serbia, without diplomatic preparation. He suggested therefore that an ultimatum to Serbia should be drawn up. His colleagues disagreed, regarding a diplomatic victory over Serbia as not worth having. The meeting decided to work for a 'speedy settlement of the conflict with Serbia by warlike

Left: Everyday life in Vienna—the high street; a servant girl asks her embarrassed upper-class lover, 'When will you marry me?' (top left); a row of typical Viennese fiakrs (bottom left)

81

or by peaceful means', and that 'mobilisation should take place only after concrete demands have been placed before and rejected by Serbia'.

Austria could rely on German support, but was unsure of the reaction of the other European powers. Not much more was known in Vienna than that in St Petersburg, Sazanov became excited at the news, and in London Sir Edward Grey had calmly proposed direct consultations between Russia and Austria. Despite this uncertainty, Austria eventually decided to act against Serbia. Tisza's doubts were finally resolved, and the terms of the ultimatum to Serbia were agreed upon.

Late in the afternoon of Thursday, 23rd July 1914 the Austrian Minister to Belgrade came to the Foreign Ministry and presented the Austrian ultimatum. Pašić, the Premier, was away from the capital and his deputy was at first reluctant to accept it. After they had read it, the Serbian ministers were convinced that they had no other choice than to fight it out. The ultimatum contained a summary of the findings against the assassins of the Archduke Franz Ferdinand and it allowed only forty-eight hours for the Serb government to comply with its ten conditions. It stated that 'The history of the last few years and the sad events of 28th June have proved the existence of a subversive movement in Serbia, the aim of which is the detachment of certain territories from Austria-Hungary. This movement, which originated in full view of the Serbian government, found its expression on this side of the frontier in a number of terrorist acts. The Serbian government not only did not respect the formal obligations of the declaration of 31st March 1909, it did nothing to suppress this movement.' The reply by the Serbian government was described as 'unsatisfactory', and war on Serbia was declared on 28th July 1914.

The rulers in Vienna delivered the future of their state into the hands of the military at a time when its internal political situation was unsettled. In Hungary, the opposition's hostility to Tisza was so deep that it was the only belligerent country which found it impossible to suspend its party differences and bring about a formal political truce for the duration of the war. In the Austrian part of the monarchy, the conflict between the Czechs and Germans in Bohemia had been getting sharper before the war. There were, we have seen, other disturbances among the Habsburg Slavs. The alliance with Germany, involving as it did a conflict with Russia, was as yet an untried policy, with some hidden risks.

Right: Mobs break up Serb-owned shops, Sarajevo, June 1914

The Point of No Return

In the course of the week after the declaration of war on Serbia, all the great European powers, with the exception of Italy, joined the hostilities. The Habsburg Empire faced its supreme test. Having declared war on Serbia on 28th July 1914 Austria-Hungary declared war on Russia on 6th August and on Belgium on 28th August. On 4th May 1915 Italy left the Triple Alliance and on the 23rd she declared war on Austria-Hungary. On 15th March 1916, Austria-Hungary declared war on Portugal, and on 27th August Rumania declared war on Austria-Hungary. Italy and Rumania both entered the war as the opponents of the Empire, hoping for territorial acquisitions at its expense.

The military situation, especially in the east, went in favour of the Central powers. Though Italy joined the Allies in the spring of 1915, Turkey had acceded to the Central empires in November 1914 and strengthened their hand in the Balkans. More important, it contributed to isolating Russia from her Allies: Russia fought the war on the Eastern Front with little outside help. By the end of the summer of 1915, the German and Austro-Hungarian troops had taken, in the course of their Russian offensive, some 750,000 prisoners, occupied the whole of Russian Poland, and concluded large-scale operations on the Eastern Front. The Austrians had been able to hold out, on the Isonzo Front, against the Italians. Early in October 1915 the Austrians and the Germans advanced against the Serbs across the Danube, and the Bulgarian armies crossed the frontier into southern Serbia: the operation was concluded in the winter of 1915. The Brusilov offensive, in the summer of 1916, was Russia's last real military effort and, in the process, the might of the Russian army was broken; in the autumn of the same year a swift German stroke eliminated Rumania, who had joined the Allies in August 1916. The Central empires gained the rich Rumanian sources of grain and oil, and the Russians had to hold an additional 300 miles of frontline.

Left: The aged Emperor inspects his unruly Bohemian provinces

Nevertheless, towards the end of 1916, the effects of the Allied blockade started making themselves felt, especially in Austria. The tensions between the two parts of the monarchy were also growing. The Hungarians were exporting less and less food to Austrian parts of the monarchy, and there were severe food shortages in the Austrian industrial districts. An Austrian politician remarked that he could have forgiven the Allies' economic blockade, but not the Hungarians'. The economic ties which, before the war, had bound the two parts of the monarchy together now started to snap.

At the beginning, neither Austria nor Hungary manifested any popular movement against the war. In Hungary, where the Liberals had been reconstituted as the Party of Work, Tisza was well supported politically. The Coalition of National Parties, led at the time by Albert Apponyi, was opposed to Tisza's policies, but welcomed the advent of the war for its own purposes. It offered to join a national cabinet with the Liberals if Tisza stood down. Tisza refused, and the Hungarians failed to achieve a formal political truce, like the *Burgfrieden* of the Germans or the *union sacrée* of the French. The Croats were more divided than the Hungarians. When their Diet met after the outbreak of the war members of the Serbo-Croat Coalition sat in silence while adherents of the Party of Law – the *pravaši* led by Ivo Frank – made fierce attacks on Serbia, an echo of violent anti-Serb riots in the towns almost everywhere in the South Slav territories.

The Austrian Germans welcomed the war as well, and there was some show of pleasure in Vienna after its outbreak. The Social Democrats had to abandon preparations for another international conference and were obliged to come to terms with the war. They were greatly helped by Russia's involvement. For many decades before August 1914, they had regarded the Tsarist regime as the most contemptible form of government and Russia as the fortress of European reaction. Now there was a chance to destroy it. Like their comrades in Germany, the Austrian Social Democrats were glad of the opportunity. The Austrian German nationalists expected the war to make up for their losses in peacetime. They wanted to strengthen their position in Austria, and regarded the war as a struggle between the Teuton and the Slav in which they were sure of victory. It was an attitude first expressed by the German Chancellor, but more strongly felt in Austria than Germany. In the Habsburg Empire the Russian Front was of absorbing interest, with the newspapers often strengthening the popular feeling that the Western Front did not really exist. The Poles also gave

Right: Conscription in Budapest met little resistance at first

their support to the war and the monarchy, deciding that Russia was their chief enemy.

As in the other countries at war, the war brought about considerable constitutional changes in Austria-Hungary. Imperial edicts took the place of the civil law code, especially in sections relating to civil liberties. 'Extraordinary Criminal Senates' replaced the criminal courts and their juries. The Imperial edict of 24th July 1914 had taken high treason, offences against members of the ruling House, disturbances of public order, revolt, and acts of sabotage away from the jurisdiction of civil courts and handed them over to the military legal machinery. In the 'military zones', the hinterland of the battlelines, the military exercised full administrative powers.

In Budapest the parliament went on meeting throughout the war, and the government often successfully resisted the growing taste of the military for civil powers. In Austria, on the other hand, the parliament was not in session at the outbreak of the war and was not convened again until May 1917. The Premier, Count Stürgkh, had not the courage to reopen the *Reichsrat* or to resist the military. His fears that parliament would become the scene of anti-war and anti-Habsburg demonstrations prevented him from fully realising what effect his decision would have on the politicians. Nor did he take into account the atmosphere of alienation in the provincial towns, particularly in Slav territories. These claustrophobic, rumour-ridden cities, where the military was often able to exercise almost unlimited powers, and where links with Vienna were strained to the utmost, became the real centres of dissent within the Empire.

In the weeks after the outbreak of war, however, there was no open revolt, even in the case of the Czechs. Nevertheless, the military authorities undertook systematic persecution of the Czechs and other Slavs. At the end of September 1914, Václav Klofáč, the National Socialist leader, was arrested and many hundreds of Ruthenes and Serbs in the war zones were arrested and executed. In Bohemia and Croatia, far from the front, a sharp contest for political power developed between the military and civil authorities.

The War Supervisory Office, created soon after the outbreak of the war, was the main instrument of the Supreme Army Command in its contest with the civil authorities. Set up to protect the armed forces against internal and external enemies, it maintained close interest in every branch of civil administration. Its extensive network of agents was well paid but unreliable.

Above: *Enlisted soldiers march cheerfully through Vienna's streets.* **Below:** *Austrian cavalry occupy Belgrade, October 1914*

The Commander-in-Chief of the armed forces, Archduke Friedrich, tried to convince both Tisza and Stürgkh that civilian authorities in the Slav districts should be replaced by military administration. Tisza, however, disapproved of the Supervisory Office and severely limited its activities on Hungarian territory. Stürgkh, because he was certain neither of himself nor of the attitudes of the Austrian Slavs to the monarchy, did not interfere.

Czech colours and drunken troops

The fight with the military in Austria therefore rested with the heads of the local administration, the men on the spot. In Prague, the Governor of Bohemia faced the severest task. The conflict flared up after incidents which occurred during the leave-taking on 22nd and 23rd September 1914, of the Eighth and the Twenty-eighth Prague Regiments. These two regiments had been recruited from districts where the National Socialist Party organisation was strong and had spent the last years before the war under the influence of powerful pro-Russian propaganda. Drunken troops were accompanied by women and children, and the disorderly procession wound its way to the railway station, singing patriotic songs. Many troops wore the Czech colours and somebody carried a red flag with the inscription: 'We are marching against the Russians and we don't know why.'

Incidents arising out of the distribution of the Russian leaflets were, however, more widespread and serious. Whereas the Poles took little notice of the proclamation by Grand Duke Nikolai Nikolaevich, the Supreme Commander of the Russian army, which, on the Tsar's behalf, offered them a new and better Poland, the later addresses to the Ruthenes and the Czechs found more response. The proclamation to the Ruthenes was a continuation of the crude, semi-religious propaganda from the years before the war. Originating from the Pochaev monastery, it read: 'Our dear brothers who suffer under the German yoke! The Holy Mother of God has heard your prayers and she will reunite you with the Orthodox Russian Empire. In the name of the Son, the Father, and the Holy Ghost, renounce your involuntary allegiance to the Austrian Emperor....' An Austrian leaflet, signed by Franz Joseph, expressed surprise that the Tsar had stooped so low as to use religion for political ends; a few Ruthenes on whom the Russian declaration was found were shot.

On 16th September 1914 Grand Duke Nikolai Nikolaevich published another declaration, this time addressed to all the Slav peoples of the Habsburg Empire. They

Right: Germany backs her partner's action — Berliners demonstrate their loyal support for Franz Joseph, July 1914

first reached north Bohemia, where they were distributed among the troops; in December 1914 a big consignment of the leaflets reached Prague. By then, however, thirty-one arrests had been made in Prague alone; by the end of the year, the number of arrests made in connection with the Russian leaflets reached several hundred.

In April 1915, another proof of Czech. treason was delivered into the hands of the military. After a battle near Dukla, one of the principal Carpathian passes, only 20 officers and 236 troops slowly reassembled of the 2,000 men of whom the Twenty-eighth Prague Regiment had originally consisted – the rest of them had been captured by the Russians. The incident became the subject of a sharp controversy in the Austro-Hungarian army. On the whole, opinion at the senior officer level inclined to the view that it was a voluntary capture. The Commander-in-Chief of the armed forces asked the Emperor to dissolve the regiment: his request was granted on 17th April 1915.

Again the campaign by the military for the complete take-over of the administration in the Slav provinces was reopened and again it failed. The soldiers retained the powers transferred to them on the outbreak of the war, but that was all. As the failures of the opening phases of the war were replaced by military success, and as the soldiers became more confident, they were less insistent on an extension of their powers. By this time, however, they had already done much harm. The use they had made of their powers during the first year of the war had alienated important sections of Slavs from the monarchy, while the insecurity and fear of the provincial towns eventually gave rise to positive and organised anti-Habsburg movements.

The violence of the war largely submerged the terrorist movement in Bosnia Herzegovina, and it was from Dalmatia and Istria on the Adriatic coast that the new leadership of the South Slav anti-Habsburg movement came. Here, the influence of Italian civilisation preserved memories of the Italian struggle for unity, and provided the South Slavs with an example to follow. In May 1915, the South Slav Committee was founded in Paris. It aimed to unite South Slav exiles everywhere and to recruit volunteers for the Serbian army, and its propaganda tried to emphasise that the Slavs were a potential fifth column within the Habsburg state.

The leaders of the South Slav Committee in exile were completely cut off from the political developments in their own country: their fortunes depended on the military success of Serbia. The Czech anti-Habsburg movement

Right: German and Austrian troops advance towards the east

also grew faster abroad than in Austria-Hungary, though it had originated in Prague. Before his arrest on 21st May 1915 Karel Kramář, while seeing to it that the public activities of his party did not exceed the obligatory declarations of loyalty to the monarchy, organised a small anti-Habsburg group inside his own party. Kramář believed in the victory of Russia and her early occupation of the Czech lands; in December 1914 he re-established contact with his old Russian friend, Svatkovski.

Like Kramář, Professor Thomas Masaryk realised the need to maintain his contacts outside the Habsburg monarchy after the outbreak of the war. The only deputy from the Realist Party in the *Reichsrat,* his standing in Czech politics owed more to the strength of his own personality than to that of his party. Born in 1850, Masaryk became the first professor of philosophy at the new Czech university in Prague. It was in 1891 that he was elected a member of the *Reichsrat,* and from then on he gave most of his time to politics, becoming involved in all the important controversies of his time. He tried to avoid chauvinism in his politics, and questioned the extreme attitudes of many of his compatriots. Masaryk was not uncritically pro-Russian, and in 1912 he stated that 'the system known as Tsarism I hate not only as a man but also as a politician and a Slav'. Such attitudes created a wide gulf between Masaryk and Kramář. In the years immediately before the war, Masaryk attempted to link the Czech question with the problem of small nations in Europe rather than basing his plans on an alliance with Russia.

When the war broke out Masaryk was sixty-four years old, very agile and ready to act. He had the advantage of not being suspect to the Austro-Hungarian authorities because he was known not to have entertained pro-Russian sympathies. He was able to travel freely to neutral countries after the outbreak of war. He visited Holland in September and October, and met R.W.Seton-Watson on his second trip. The Austrian press offered little information of value about events abroad and in the front lines, and Masaryk was keen to discover more, being prepared, in return, to release information on Austro-Hungarian affairs. The war, in his view, far from being a clash between the Teuton and the Slav, was rather a vehicle of far-reaching political, social, and moral change. It was a struggle in which, he was convinced, the British Empire would play a vital part.

The Young Czech group kept their anti-Habsburg conspiracy very much to themselves; Masaryk and his associates, on the other hand, welcomed the opinions of

Left: Austrian soldiers tend the wounded on the Italian Front

other political parties. Eduard Beneš, a young teacher who later developed the manner and mind of the perfect private secretary, was one of Masaryk's most devoted followers. He kept in touch with the Social Democrat leader, Bohumiř Šmeral. When Beneš talked to him on 3rd November 1914, the Social Democrat told him that, according to his information from Berlin, it was possible that a separate peace would be made between Germany and Russia, and that Russia was a very unreliable party in the war.

Kramář's pre-war plan was for a Slav confederation, while Masaryk planned for an independent state. It was to contain, apart from the Czech lands, the Slovak provinces of Hungary. It was to be a kingdom — Masaryk was not yet a republican — with a Western, preferably Danish or Belgian, prince on the throne, rather than a Russian Archduke. Masaryk knew that without a decisive defeat of Germany there would be no independent Czechoslovak state. Having developed his plans and consulted some Czech and South Slav politicians, he left for Rome on 18th December 1914. In February 1915, when Beneš visited Masaryk in Switzerland, they decided to set up a secret committee in Prague 'on the lines of Russian revolutionary practice', which would keep in touch with the exiles and at the same time influence the politicians at home. When Beneš returned to Prague he persuaded Kramář to co-operate with him, and a small anti-Habsburg group was established in Prague.

By the end of the winter of 1914-15 the Russians, resisting the advances of the Germans and Austrians, moved forward into Galicia and Bukovina. Kramář was convinced that the Russian advance would continue. For that reason the anti-Habsburg Czechs refused to join Masaryk in exile: they preferred instead to wait for the arrival of the Russian army. Kramář eventually succeeded in persuading one pro-Russian Agrarian deputy, Josef Dürich, to go abroad. Dürich caused trouble for Masaryk by working exclusively towards Slav federation and encouraging the groups of Czech immigrants in Russia to do the same. There had been sharp differences between the Czechs and Slovaks in the West and in America on the one hand, and the Czechs in Russia on the other as to the shape of the future state. They were resolved only in 1917, when Masaryk gained control of the immigrant societies and Russia left the war.

In the meantime Masaryk was joined by Beneš in September 1915, and, helped by his French and English friends, set out to publicise the cause of Czech and Slovak independence in the Allied countries in the West.

Right: Franz Joseph, the last great Habsburg ruler, is buried

It was a difficult task: the public in England and France were unfamiliar with the peoples of Austria-Hungary and their political ambitions, and the politicians were unmoved by them. For the time being nobody seemed interested in putting an end to the Habsburg Empire.

A year later, however, events moved forward. On 21st October 1916, Friedrich Adler, the son of the leader of the Austrian Social Democrats, assassinated Stürgkh, the Prime Minister. Adler thought of his deed as a 'demonstration visible from afar', a protest against the repressive government of Stürgkh. At the beginning of November, the Emperor fell ill with bronchial catarrh. Though he continued to get up and work as usual until 21st November, on that day he asked for an armchair to be brought to his writing desk. He died the same evening, after the administration of extreme unction.

He was succeeded by Karl I, his grandnephew, the son of Archduke Otto. Karl was not yet thirty years old; he was married to Zita, Princess of Bourbon-Parma. Although he had held military commands in the war, he had virtually no political experience on his succession: his only assets were charm and a willingness to experiment. At a difficult time of the war he succeeded one of the strongest of the Habsburg rulers, the personification of a whole era, of the whole Empire. His own personality was unremarkable, and his enemies said that he was too much under the influence of his wife on whom he usually relied for judgment of other people's characters. When he was crowned as Charles IV of Hungary, the Crown of St Stephen came down over his eyes.

On 23rd December 1916, Ottokar, Count Czernin, became the Foreign Minister. Czernin had been, since 1905, a close associate of the late Archduke Franz Ferdinand, and shared his political views on the reorganisation of the monarchy. In particular he believed that the creation of a third constituent part of the monarchy – in addition to Austria-Hungary – would solve the problem of the South Slavs. Czernin became Ambassador to Bucharest in 1913 and was generally regarded as a successful diplomat, though in 1916 he failed to keep Rumania neutral. When he became Foreign Minister he put his trust in the Emperor just as he had put it in Archduke Franz Ferdinand before the war. Like the Emperor, Czernin believed that an immediate peace must be made.

He was even more pessimistic than the German Ambassador to Vienna about the desperate position of the Habsburg monarchy; his views on the need for peace were strengthened by the events in Russia in March

Right: Serbia, intent on resisting the Empire, is stabbed in the back by Bulgaria, who sides with the Central powers, 1915

1917. Bread riots in Petrograd grew into a revolution which forced first the government and then the Tsar from their positions of power: unlike the 1905 Revolution, which was swiftly suppressed by the army, no government agency was able to deal successfully with the revolutionaries in 1917. Czernin wrote to his Emperor that '. . . the amazing facility with which the strongest monarchy in the world was overthrown contributes to our anxiety and calls to memory the saying *exemplae trahunt*. . . . The revolution affects our Slavs more than the Germans, and the responsibility for the continuation of the war is a far greater one for a monarch whose country is only united through the dynasty than for one where the peoples themselves are fighting for their national ideals.' Measures were taken to show the Slavs the good will of the government: the *Reichsrat* was reconvened in May 1917, and an amnesty for political prisoners was declared.

The Emperor seeks peace

By then, the Emperor had taken the first steps to give his peoples peace. In February 1917, two brothers of Empress Zita, both of them officers in the Belgian army, had visited their sister and brother-in-law in Austria. The Emperor revealed his desire for peace to them and, in the spring, addressed two letters to the elder of them, Prince Sixtus, on the subject. In the first letter he mentioned the 'justified claims' of France to Alsace-Lorraine; in the second he wrongly alleged that Italy had given up her territorial claims. Sixtus had met Czernin on one occasion but did not consult with the Foreign Minister on the contents of these letters. The Habsburg Court and Prince Sixtus thought in terms of a separate peace, which a general peace would somehow follow. The Foreign Minister, on the other hand, always remained scrupulously loyal to the German alliance.

Czernin's own emissaries worked on his instructions. Count Mensdorff, the former Ambassador to Washington, left for Denmark in the spring of 1917 hoping to pave the way for a general peace. But after several weeks' travelling in and out of Scandinavian capitals, he had to admit failure and return to Vienna. Sir Francis Hopgood, who was sent to meet him, had little experience in diplomatic negotiations, nor was he in the position to make any undertakings. A meeting was finally arranged in Geneva in November 1917, between Mensdorff and General Smuts. During the two days' exchange of views – the most open conversation between the two opposed parties during the war – the nature of their misunderstanding was soon revealed. Smuts wanted a separate peace with Austria, thinking that this was what the Austrians wanted;

Mensdorff, acting on the instructions of Czernin and not of the Emperor, was preparing the ground for a general peace. In any case, the Italian government, ever since it had first been told about the possibility of a peace with Austria in April 1917, had bitterly opposed it.

In the meantime, on the Austrian side, hopes for a victory in the war had started to rise. A few days before Smuts and Mensdorff met, the Bolshevik Revolution had taken place. Russia was eliminated from the war as a factor to be reckoned with: since late summer, the Germans had been extracting their troops from the Eastern Front. Czernin was right when he said that the Russian Revolution would have a strong impact on the Habsburg monarchy, especially on the Slavs. On 19th May 1917, shortly before the reopening of the *Reichsrat,* a newspaper in Prague published *The Manifesto of Czech Writers,* with its first 150 signatures. It asked the deputies to be the 'true spokesmen of their own nation' and concluded: 'A democratic Europe, consisting of autonomous and free states, is the Europe of the future. The nation demands, gentlemen, that you should rise to this historic occasion and that you act as free and independent men, without any regard to personal advantages, men of supreme moral and national conscience. If you cannot act according to the demands of the nation . . . give up your mandates before you enter the parliament.'

The Manifesto heralded a change in the attitude of the Czech politicians to the monarchy. When the Entente, in its reply, on 10th January 1917, to President Wilson's war aims enquiry, had made a passing reference to the 'liberation of the Czechoslovaks', Czech deputies handed over to Czernin a declaration, which described the Entente remark as an 'insinuation'. It pointed out that the 'Czech people as always in the past, in the present and future as well, sees its future and the conditions of its development only under the sceptre of the Habsburgs'. All that began to change in the spring of 1917. In April 1917, Masaryk and Beneš sent a detailed list of instructions to the Czech politicians from Paris, drawing their attention 'to the success we have achieved here', and asking them not to take the existence of Austria-Hungary for granted: 'Remember there is a revolution in Russia and that they will have a republic there.' The prisoners — Kramář and Klofáč among them — were amnestied, and returned to political life, and so did the deputies who had served in the army. After the publication of the Writers' Manifesto, Czech members in the *Reichsrat* worked out a compromise. They assumed that the Habs-

Left: Coronation of Emperor Karl and wife as King and Queen of Hungary, December 1916. With them, Crown Prince Otto

burg monarchy would continue to exist, but made a sharp attack on the monarchy's internal arrangements. They criticised the dual system of government because, in their view, it had led to the emergence of ruling and subject peoples in the monarchy; they demanded its transformation into a federal state, including a state of the Czechs and the Slovaks. Two Czech deputies, however, disassociated themselves from the majority programme, and demanded the formation of an independent Czechoslovak state.

When they put their programme before the opening meeting of the parliament on 30th May 1917, it caused great consternation. The Premier asked the chairman of the club of the Czech deputies to withdraw it, but he refused to do so. The Czechs were by no means isolated in the parliament. In March 1917 they had agreed with the South Slav deputies on a united approach to constitutional problems. On 30th May 1917, a Slovene member told the *Reichsrat* that 'we demand the unification of all the lands inhabited by the Slovenes, Croats, and Serbs of the monarchy in one autonomous state, free from all foreign domination, ruled in a democratic manner under the Habsburg sceptre'. Like the Czechs, he was striking at the very roots of the dual system.

The position of the Poles was more difficult. Divided among Germany, Russia, and Austria-Hungary and fighting the war on two sides, they could neither win nor lose it. However, they could work for the unification of their country. Josef Piłsudski and the Polish Legion had been fighting on the Austro-Hungarian side since the beginning; in the summer offensive in 1915, the whole of Poland passed under the control of the Central empires, with whom political initiative now therefore lay. The result was the Two Emperors' Manifesto on 5th November 1916 — one of Franz Joseph's last political acts — a compromise with Berlin achieved after long and acrimonious diplomatic exchanges. The Germans at first made no objections to the 'Austro-Polish' solution, which proposed a more or less united Poland (there existed little hope that Germany would give up its part of the country; the plan therefore involved Austrian and Russian Poland only) in a personal union with the Habsburg dominions. Berlin's only concern was that a premature declaration concerning Russian Poland should not jeopardise the hopes of a separate peace with St Petersburg.

When the Germans changed their minds and opposed that plan, the Austrians found it hard to come to terms with the new situation. The Two Emperors' Manifesto provided for an autonomous Poland, but concerned only the former Congress Kingdom, i.e. the Russian part of it. On the day of the publication of the Manifesto, Franz

Joseph wrote to the German Prime Minister, informing him of his intention to confer a higher degree of autonomy on Galicia. The Germans did not like the proposal, and suspected the Austrians of plotting to win as much influence in the autonomous state as they could.

Nevertheless, the plans for the unification of Poland were gaining ground. After the revolution in Russia, Roman Dmowski, a Polish deputy to the Russian Duma before 1912, founded the Polish National Council in Paris, which propagated the idea of an independent and united Poland in the Western Allied countries, and in America. The Austrian Poles, who had been disappointed with the Two Emperors' Manifesto, declared, when the *Reichsrat* reassembled in May 1917, that their club would soon comment on the national problems of the Empire in the light of the Kraków agreement made on 28th May 1917. It had formulated the demand for a united and independent Poland.

Though the differences between the Old Ruthene and the Ukrainian movements became submerged in the war, the conflict between the Ukrainians and the Poles was growing sharper. In May 1917 the Ukrainians came out with their view of Galicia as an 'artificial administrative unit' and went on to 'welcome the endeavour of the Ukrainians in Russia for the achievement of the right of self-determination'. A Ukrainian state then emerged from the peace negotiations between the Central powers and Russia in February 1918. It contained none of the east Galician districts, but was given the former Polish-Russian province of Kholm. The Poles of Austria never forgave their Vienna government for being a party to that agreement.

As the Russian Revolution developed in the course of the year 1917, its impact in Austria-Hungary changed. It first stimulated national, then social demands. Its undertones were pacifist throughout. After the failure of the last Russian offensive (mounted by the revolutionary provisional government in the summer of 1917) all was quiet on the Eastern Front. The Russian side was slowly melting away. In December 1917 peace negotiations between Lenin's government and the Central Powers got under way. They had made little progress by mid-January 1918 when Trotsky, the Soviet Commissar of Foreign Affairs, started using them for revolutionary propaganda (the negotiations received a lot of publicity) rather than for the conclusion of a peace treaty with the Central Powers.

Lenin and Trotsky were partly successful. Though no general European revolution put an end to the war, the

Left: Ottokar Czernin, the Austrian Foreign Minister (right)

impact of their propaganda was stronger in Austria-Hungary than anywhere else. The winter of 1917-18 was especially severe and economically even more disastrous than the previous one. On 11th January 1918, the Governor of Bohemia wrote to his friend Czernin, who was then at the head of the Austro-Hungarian delegation to Brest-Litovsk: 'I do not doubt that you have been informed by the Austrian government about the level of our corn reserves up to the next harvest. But judging by the impressions I had in Vienna I doubt that you know the whole truth, that we are faced with a catastrophe which will hit us in the next few weeks, unless we receive foreign help at the last moment. The reserves in Bohemia will last until the middle of April, but only if Bohemia does not have to supply anyone else. The situation in other crown-lands is much worse; starvation has already begun there. . . .'

Three days later food rations were reduced in Austria, and workers' demonstrations took place in the industrial districts around Vienna. In the following two days some 95,000 men came out on strike in Lower Austria and, on 18th January 1918, the movement spread to Budapest. A large part of Hungary's industry came to a standstill. The strike paralysed Hungarian railways; workers' Soviets, on the Russian pattern, were elected at several large factories. Nevertheless, the strength and the political form of the strike movement varied from district to district. Whereas in Austria and Hungary it tended to be wild, uncontrolled by the Social Democrat party leadership, and with strong social undertones, in the industrial areas of Bohemia and Moravia it was, with a few exceptions, a movement divided by the Social Democrat movement, which advanced specific national demands. (In the course of the year 1917, the leadership of the Czech Social Democracy gradually abandoned its loyal pro-Habsburg position. It was able to channel working class discontent in national rather than social revolution.) Nevertheless, the Austro-Hungarian troops, reinforced by the units released from the Russian Front, were able to bring the situation under control. The hopes of the Bolshevik leaders in Petrograd for a revolution flickered, and died out.

Early in 1918, the Central Powers were victorious in the east. They first concluded peace with the Ukraine, then with Russia; and finally with Rumania. The influence of Germany in Central and Eastern Europe culminated in the conclusion of those treaties, and affected the enemies of Berlin as well as its allies.

From the beginning of the war, the anti-Habsburg

Left: Hungarian nationalism threatens to oust Emperor Karl

exiles had maintained that Austria-Hungary was in Germany's tow, that she was ordered about and used by Berlin without a murmur of protest. There were, in actual fact, sharp differences between Vienna and Berlin. Soon after the outbreak of the hostilities in August 1914, the Austrians accused the Germans of letting them look after more than their fair share of the Russian Front. The German Ambassador to Vienna was convinced that the government of Austria-Hungary was acting in the 'spirit of Sadowa', and made frequent reference to it in his dispatches. The views of the two allies clashed sharply on subjects ranging from the proper use of the Turkish armed forces to the settlement of the future of Poland. The two states were far from being one.

In spring 1918 an opportunity arose for Berlin to bring the Austrians to heel. On 2nd April Czernin made an unwise reference to Clemenceau, the French Premier. It elicited an explosive reply. Clemenceau revealed the efforts of Emperor Karl and his brother-in-law, Prince Sixtus, to make a separate peace. Czernin resigned and the Emperor was summoned to Spa, the seat of the German General HQ. On 8th May 1918, the Kaiser and Emperor Karl signed an agreement which bound closely the Austrian and German Empires. It provided for the formation of a military and customs union and for the 'conclusion of a long-term and close political alliance between the two Empires for their defence and security'. The fact that time was fast running out was the only thing that prevented the agreement from being implemented.

When it was signed, the Germans still held the initiative on the Western Front. They had opened their great offensive on 21st March 1918, which on several occasions threatened to divide the English sector of the front from the French. It brought Paris within the reach of the German guns and almost 250,000 Allied prisoners were taken. The United States had come into the war almost a year before the beginning of the offensive, but when it began American forces employed at the front were still negligible. The German victory in the east and their offensive in the west, as well as the unrelieved situation on the Italian front (the Austrian offensive in the autumn of 1917 had broken through the Italian lines) put Britain and France into a desperate position. The possibility of German victory was thus in the air in the spring of 1918.

Left: Distributing bread to queuing women in Vienna, late 1917. The Allied blockade caused severe shortage in Austria after 1916 and simultaneously Hungary exported less and less

Chapter 6

The Final Collapse

Against this background the Allies made the decision to break up the Habsburg Empire. In the spring of 1917 the Czech and South Slav politicians in the *Reichsrat* had demanded the transformation of Austria-Hungary into a federal state. We know that the exiles in the Allied countries had been working for the dissolution of the Empire and the formation of independent states. We have examined the way in which the phases of the Russian Revolution affected political developments in Central and Eastern Europe. But Lenin's Russia left the ranks of the warring powers: the war had broken her military strength. From now on for several years she would turn in on herself, occupied with her own problems. The hopes of the South Slav, or Czech, or Ruthene pro-Russian politicians had vanished with Russia's defeat. Apart from the views and actions of its own peoples, the future of the Habsburg Empire depended on the decisions taken in London and Paris, Washington and Rome.

The revolution in Russia and the entry of America into the war had put into circulation the doctrine of self-determination of peoples — that is the freedom to form their own independent states — and it was confirmed by President Wilson's Fourteen Points, published in January 1918. It was not specified whether autonomy or complete independence was the more appropriate gift for the Habsburg peoples, but unity and independence were promised to the Poles. Early in 1918 the Czech and South Slav exiles still had no specific promise from any of the Allied governments. Reference had been made to the liberation of the Czechoslovaks in January 1917, but that was all. Throughout that year, the exiles had faced the gravest danger: the possibility of the conclusion of a separate peace with Austria-Hungary. That was why, in his messages to Prague, Beneš insisted that it should not be taken for granted that the Habsburg state would continue to exist for ever, and therefore that it should be recognised that its peoples, rather than its government, had the

Left: 'Beware!' — *poster of the infant Hungarian state warns members of the old regime against attempting to overthrow it*

right to negotiate. By the end of the year the danger of a separate peace had disappeared, and the possibility of German victory loomed ahead.

The anti-Habsburg exiles had been recruiting troops since the early months of the war, and in some cases set up their own units. Polish, South Slav, and Czech troops — both pre-war immigrants and political exiles who left the monarchy after the outbreak of the war — fought on the Entente side on all the major battlelines of the First World War. The Czech Legion in Russia consisted largely of immigrants, and had been sanctioned by the Tsarist authorities in the autumn of 1914. We have seen that before the revolution in Russia, the conflict between the Russian and Masaryk's anti-Habsburg movements culminated in an attempt to establish a rival Czechoslovak political centre in Petrograd. (Masaryk's National Committee was based on Paris.) The Russian government, desiring to unite 'all Czech elements loyal to Russia', supported the attempt.

The Russian revolution frustrated those plans. Professor Paul Milyukov, who had known Masaryk since before the war, became Foreign Minister in the first provisional government. The pro-Tsarist societies of Czech immigrants lost their prestige and influence, and their place was taken by the organisations of prisoners of war who welcomed the revolution and supported Masaryk's leadership. On 16th May 1917 Masaryk himself came to Petrograd, in order to unite the Czech organisations under his leadership and to convince the Russian authorities to allow the prisoners of war to join the Czech Legion. In July 1917, the way to a 'Czechoslovak army, as big as possible', was open. By the end of the year it was about 40,000 men strong.

The political transfiguration of the Czech movement in Russia — from devotion to the Tsar and his State to enthusiasm for the revolution — was fast, but not fast enough. Masaryk linked the Czechoslovak movement to the moderate, middle-class element in the revolution. The Czechoslovak brigade had attacked enemy lines in the disastrous Kerensky offensive in the summer of 1917, while the Russian troops on its flanks were deserting the front. When Lenin's Bolsheviks, the extreme pacifist section of the revolutionary movement took over its leadership in November 1917, Masaryk's Czechoslovaks were again isolated.

Masaryk left Moscow for the United States on 8th March 1918, after agreements had been made with France on the transfer of the Czechoslovak troops to the

Right: Piłsudski, who worked actively for Polish independence, leads the Polish Legion into Russian Poland in August 1914

Western Front via Siberia, and with the Bolshevik government on their free passage, on the Trans-Siberian railway, to Vladivostok. The Czechs started leaving European Russia on their journey east. But there were difficulties with the Bolsheviks about the amount of arms the Czechs were allowed and early in May 1918, an open conflict between them flared up. The Allied governments had been considering intervention in Russia as a means of reconstituting the Eastern Front: the clash between the Czechs and the Bolsheviks speeded up their plans. The Czech brigade, strung out along the Trans-Siberian railway, became an important factor in the Allied policy of intervention in Russia.

The National Committee in Paris, which was run by Beneš in Masaryk's absence, abandoned plans for the transfer of the Czechoslovak brigade to the Western Front. On 1st April 1918 Beneš received a message from the French Military Attaché in London saying that there were difficulties with transport and that it was doubtful whether the brigade could reach the Western Front. Beneš was undismayed by this note and remarked that as a document it was 'of historical interest. It inaugurated our politically important negotiations about the army, which I used for our political recognition in France and in England.'

Pressure to end the Empire

Pressure on the Allied governments and the United States to put an end to the Habsburg Empire came from several directions. There was the pressure of military necessity, the publicity put out by the exiles and their persuasiveness about the rightness of their cause, and finally the opinion of experts. The strongest pressure-group of experts was based in London: they protected the government from too much direct contact with the exiles, although they were all, more or less, under the exiles' influence and committed to their plans. R.W. Seton-Watson worked for the Foreign Office and then, together with Wickham Steed (*The Times*'s man in Vienna before the war); he assisted Lord Northcliffe who was the director of propaganda in enemy territories, a department of Beaverbrook's Ministry of Information. Lewis Namier, the Polish-born historian, spent most of the war writing memoranda on Central and Eastern Europe.

The experts were all agreed that the Habsburg Empire must be broken up. In a memorandum for Northcliffe, drafted in February 1918, Steed pointed out the military advantages of the policy of encouraging revolutionary nationalism in the Habsburg Empire. However, in their

Right: The Czech Legion is organised from Kiev by Masaryk

many memoranda and other written work for the government, the experts did not bother to point out how difficult it would be to construct nation states in Central and Eastern Europe, owing to its heterogeneous national composition, nor did they analyse the social implications of the break-down of the established order.

While deliberations about intervention in Russia were still going on at the Supreme HQ in Paris, the Allies sanctioned the break-up of the Habsburg Empire in practice. Steed left for Italy in the middle of March 1918, where he soon found out that the Italian intelligence officers were in agreement with him on the best means of lowering the morale of the enemy troops. The Italians suggested that the national committees of the exiles should proclaim their peoples' independence, and that the Allied governments should 'authorise' the proclamations. Northcliffe consented and the propaganda offensive on the Italian front went into action early in April 1918.

In the spring and summer of 1918 communication between the Czech politicians abroad and Prague was again functioning smoothly, and Beneš kept up a steady flow of news about the successes he and Masaryk were having abroad. Early in July Beneš described the 'greatest political success we have had so far'; on 29th June 1918, Pichon, the French Foreign Minister, had addressed to him a letter recognising the Czechoslovak National Committee 'publicly and officially, as the highest organ embodying the interests of the nation, and as the first basis of the future Czechoslovak government'. Beneš told the politicians in Prague that he assumed that the other part of the government was to be found among them, and dwelt on the importance of their co-operating with his and Masaryk's Committee. The Poles — though their national movement was still more fragmented than the Czechs' — also knew that the end of the war would bring them their own united state.

At that point, early in the summer of 1918, the fortunes of the war started to turn. After four months, the German offensive on the Western Front had spent itself, more American units started taking up their positions, and the initiative passed into the hands of the Allies. On the Italian front as well, the Austrian offensive in June started grinding to a halt. Finally, on 15th September 1918, Allied armies attacked, from Salonika, on the Bulgarian front. Ludendorff's plan of negotiating a favourable peace while withdrawing in the west, with his Italian and Macedonian flanks covered, was shattered. On 29th September, the German Supreme Command decided

Right: Czech exiles find support abroad — recruiting base at Stamford, Connecticut, for the Czechoslovak army in France

to appeal for an armistice: a week later, Prince Max von Baden, the new German Chancellor, asked the American President to 'arrange the immediate conclusion of an armistice on land, by sea, and in the air'.

When Foch's offensive between 26th-28th September threatened to split the German front in the west, the Austro-Hungarian army was still operating on enemy territory in Poland, Ukraine, Serbia, Rumania, and Italy. But since the beginning of the year, the morale of the Austro-Hungarian army had received a severe battering. Many of the prisoners of war who returned from Russia had been influenced by Bolshevik pacifist propaganda. At their camps in Austria-Hungary, ideological de-contamination units were set up. Whereas the transfer of German units from the Eastern to the Western Front had on the whole gone smoothly, seven Austro-Hungarian combat divisions, earmarked for the Italian front, had been used to break the January 1918 strikes. They were in fact never moved up to the front, though the High Command kept on asking for them to be returned. The situation occasioned a sharp and long exchange of view between the Chief-of-Staff and the Minister of Defence. Finally, on 8th July 1918, General Arz ordered all combat divisions to leave for the frontline. The Minister countered the order by an appeal to the Emperor. The army had to fight both internal and external enemies at the same time.

Whereas the Hungarian government managed to retain some control in its territories in the last months of the war, the government in Austria gave up its rights and duties one by one. The Slav politicians continued to attack the government in the *Reichsrat* but began to weary of this futile exercise. On 14th September, the Emperor published a peace manifesto without consulting Berlin, but no one took any notice of it. In October the Austrian Premier made the final bid to rally the politicians behind his government. In May 1917, the majority of the deputies had demanded a federal Habsburg Empire. On 16th October 1918, an Imperial Manifesto promised them a federal Austria. It did not save the State for the Habsburgs, and facilitated the transfer of power from the Austrian authorities to the local politicians. Finally, a delegation of five Czech politicians left Vienna for Geneva on 25th October. They met Beneš there and agreed that they would do nothing without the consent of Masaryk's and Beneš's Committee; Beneš on his part assured them an independent Czechoslovak state would be created, and that it would be represented at the peace conference.

The merging of the two Czech anti-Habsburg move-

Left: Czech traitors are executed by Austrian soldiers, 1918

ments—of the exiles and the politicians in Prague—sealed the fate of the Habsburg Empire. It had been recognised by both the belligerent sides early in the war that the Polish problem would have to be solved on an international level. The South Slavs had Serbia to turn to, the Habsburg Rumanians had Rumania, and the Italians had Italy. The Czechs had only their exiles' Committee. Yet the recognition of its aims, by the Allied governments as well as the Prague politicians, meant the end of the Habsburg Empire as it had existed for some three centuries. It would have mattered little to the dynasty had it given up the Italian or the Rumanian territories. The exchange of the South Slav or Polish territories for its survival could have been contemplated. But the three basic units of Austria, Bohemia and Moravia, and Hungary were the backbone of the Empire. They had made it economically viable as well as giving it its military strength. They drew other territories to them because they were strong, and they would have remained strong had they shed those territories. The triangle Vienna—Budapest—Prague was the basic fact of the Habsburg geometry. The state founded on it had the advantage of being the most powerful in south-eastern Europe, without having to suffer the discomfort of being entirely wedged between Germany and Russia.

Soon after the Czechs, the Austrians and the Hungarians started moving away from the Habsburg State. On 21st October 1918 the Austrian Germans in the *Reichsrat* formed themselves into a national assembly and on 30th October they proclaimed an independent state. On 31st October Count Károlyi formed a democratic government in Budapest, and on 3rd November announced the establishment of an independent state.

These various manifestos in October and November were no more than declarations of intention. A united state was announced in Warsaw on 6th October, but the Poles had still to create it; the Austrian State had as yet no frontiers; the Hungarians still had Slovakia in their possession, though they did not oppose the transfer of military and civil administration into the hands of South Slav politicians. The Italians, however, occupied large tracts of the Adriatic littoral early in November. The international situation was equally fluid. On 29th October 1918 *The Times* pointed out that the Allies and Americans could not deal solely with the Austro-Hungarian government (it signed the armistice) in regard to the future of the peoples of the Habsburg Empire: 'The Czecho-Slovak people is already recognised as a belli-

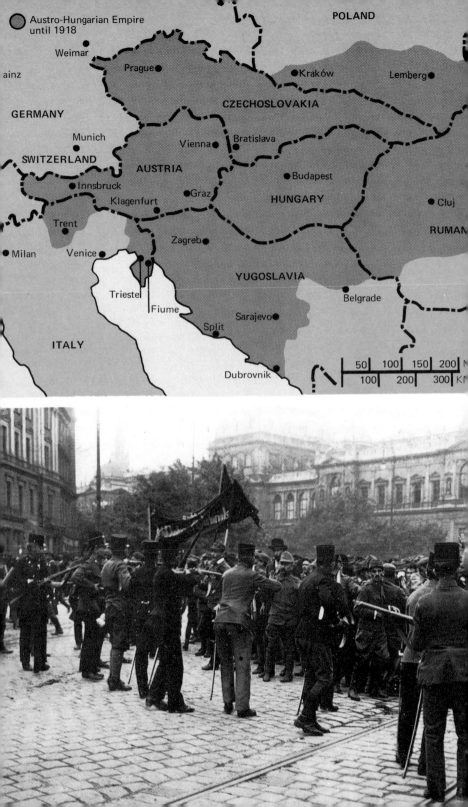

POLAND

Weimar

Prague

Kraków

Lemberg

CZECHOSLOVAKIA

ainz

GERMANY

Munich

Vienna

Bratislava

SWITZERLAND

AUSTRIA

Budapest

Innsbruck

Klagenfurt

Graz

HUNGARY

Cluj

Trent

Zagreb

RUMAN

Milan

Venice

YUGOSLAVIA

Trieste

Fiume

Belgrade

Split

Sarajevo

ITALY

Dubrovnik

50   100   150   200

100   200   300   KM

RUSSIA

harest

ARIA

gerent and Allied nation. President Wilson has recognised in the fullest manner the justice of the nationalistic aspirations of the Jugoslavs for freedom . . . the French government the National Committee of Rumanians and Transylvanian Rumanes in Paris. The Poles are also recognised. The Ruthenes may need recognition, and the Italian Austrians naturally find their champions in Italy. The right of the Austro-Hungarian "government" to speak for the German Austrians is not clear, and Count Andrássy himself can hardly have a valid mandate to represent anything save the Magyar Junker oligarchy.'

On 11th November 1918, Emperor Karl signed a document of abdication: 'Since my accession to the throne I have unceasingly tried to spare my nations the horrors of the war, for the outbreak of which I bear no responsibility. I have never hesitated to restore constitutional life, and I have opened the way for my nations to their independent political development. Since I am filled now, as before, by unchangeable love for all my nations, I will not place my person as an obstacle to their free evolution. . . .' The young Emperor and his family retired to the Eckartsau hunting lodge to the east of Vienna. They were soon to leave Austria and go into exile.

Twenty years of precarious peace followed the dissolution of the Habsburg Empire. It was less stable in Central and Eastern Europe than anywhere else on the Continent. For some time after the war, the Czechs fought the Hungarians, and the Poles defended their eastern territories against Trotsky's Red Army. There was little food for the civilian population, and the soldiers began returning home. There was social unrest everywhere and a Soviet Republic was proclaimed in Budapest. Though the peace conference on the whole satisfied the national ambitions of the former 'oppressed' peoples, it introduced new divisions in that part of Europe. Most of the successor states of the Habsburg Empire emerged on the victorious side: only Austria and Hungary were consigned to the defeated states. And when the frontiers of the states were laid down, economic barriers went up. The new order came into being under the patronage of the Western powers — France, Britain, and America — at a time when the power of both Germany and Russia suffered a temporary eclipse. Soon, the young Hitler set out to regain for the Germans their lost position, and Russia started recovering her strength — the First World War had been sparked off along the uneasy borderline between the east and the centre of Europe: so was the Second.

Top left: Map showing the final break-up of the Habsburg Empire, and the successor states. *Bottom:* 1918 — police and revolutionaries in a confrontation in front of Vienna University

Chronology of Events

1848 **3rd March:** In Budapest Kossuth denounces the Vienna system and demands responsible government for Hungary. **13th:** Metternich resigns after demonstrations in Vienna. **31st:** Emperor Franz Joseph accepts the March Laws, incorporating the Ten Points of Deák, and Hungary becomes virtually independent

1855 **18th August:** The Austrian Concordat places education, censorship, and matrimonial law under the control of the clergy

1866 **3rd July:** The Austrians are crushingly defeated at Sadowa by the Prussians, and the Seven Weeks' War comes to an end. **20th July:** They score a victory against the Italian fleet at Lissa

1867 **19th June:** Maximilian, the Emperor of Mexico, is executed. **October:** The Magyars extract a compromise from Franz Joseph whereby Austria and Hungary form the two halves of a Dual State, the person of the Emperor linking them, and common ministries of foreign affairs, war, and finance are set up

1870 **30th July:** The Habsburgs reply to the promulgation of the dogma of papal infallibility by suspending the 1855 Concordat

1872 **September:** The German, Russian, and Austro-Hungarian Emperors meet in Berlin to form the *Dreikaiserbund*

1875 **July:** There is an insurrection against Turkish rule in Herzegovina and then in Bosnia, Serbia supports the insurgents

1878 **13th June – 13th July:** The Berlin Congress, called by Bismarck, is attended by Gorchakov for Russia and Andrássy for Austria-Hungary. Austria-Hungary is given a mandate to occupy Bosnia and Herzegovina and to garrison the Sanjak of Novi Bazar

1889 **January:** The suicides of Crown Prince Rudolf and Marie Vetsera

1898 Empress Elizabeth is assassinated on the shores of Lake Geneva

1906 Introduction of universal male suffrage in the Austrian part of the monarchy

1908 **24th July:** The rising of the Young Turks under the leadership of Shevket Pasha, who in 1909 crushes the counter-revolution **5th October:** Austria-Hungary annexes Bosnia and Herzegovina

1912 **18th October:** The outbreak of the First Balkan War

1913 **29th June – 30th July:** The Second Balkan War is fought

1914 **28th June:** Archduke Franz Ferdinand and his wife are assassinated at Sarajevo. **28th July:** Austria-Hungary declares war on Serbia. **6th August:** She declares war on Russia, and on the **28th,** on Belgium.

1915 **May:** The South Slav Committee is founded in Paris and on the **23rd** Italy declares war on Austria-Hungary

1916 **27th August:** Rumania declares war on Austria-Hungary. **21st October:** Stürgkh, the Austro-Hungarian Prime Minister, is assassinated. **5th November:** The Two Emperors' Manifesto, in which the Central Powers proclaim the Kingdom of Poland, is signed. **21st:** Franz Joseph dies. He is succeeded by Karl

1917 **3rd March:** Russia signs the Treaty of Brest-Litovsk abandoning Poland, Lithuania, the Ukraine, the Baltic provinces, Finland, and Transcaucasia. **12th September:** The Central Powers grant a constitution to the former Russian Poland

1918 **28th October:** The Czechoslovaks declare their independence **3rd November:** An armistice is concluded between the Allied powers and Austria-Hungary. **7th:** Croatia and Slovenia are united to Serbia and Montenegro. **11th:** Emperor Karl abdicates and on the **12th** the Austrian Socialist Republic is declared. **16th:** The Hungarian Soviet Republic is declared. **24th:** King Peter of Serbia becomes King of the United Kingdom of the Serbs, Croats, and Slovenes at Zagreb. **1st December:** A national assembly of the Rumanians of Transylvania and the Banat at Alba Julia votes for union of these regions with Rumania

*Right: Franz Joseph the Imperial hunter (top). The ageing Emperor is attacked by death watch beetle (middle). Archduke Rudolf lies in state (bottom). **Centre:** The Emperor as father-figure; a small altar in his honour (top). The Empress Elizabeth (bottom). **Far right:** Bismarck at Sadona (top). An Italian cartoon of Austro-Hungarian threats (middle). The funeral of Franz Joseph (bottom)*

Index of main people, places, and events

Author's suggestions for further reading

A popular account of the decline of the Habsburg rule in the 19th and 20th centuries is given by Edward Crankshaw in *The Fall of the House of Habsburg* (Longman 1963), and one of the best contemporary descriptions of the Empire can be found in Geoffrey Drage's *Austria-Hungary* (John Murray 1909). C.A. Macartney's *The Habsburg Empire 1790-1918* (Weidenfeld and Nicolson 1969) forms a valuable contribution to Habsburg historiography, especially in its early part (up to 1867), and for a reliable introduction to the study of the Empire the reader should turn to A.J.May's *The Habsburg Monarchy 1867-1914* (Harvard University Press 1951).

For a more detailed history, there is May's *The Passing of the Habsburg Monarchy 1914-18* (two volumes, University of Pennsylvania Press 1966), which, however, lacks the tautness of the earlier volume. R.A.Kann's *The Multinational Empire* (two volumes, Columbia University Press 1950) is good especially on the political institutions of the Habsburg state, and H.W.Steed's *The Habsburg Monarchy* (Constable 1913) is a description of the Habsburg state and society by the correspondent of *The Times* in Vienna who disapproved of the old order.

The works of R.W.Seton-Watson, a pioneer of Habsburg studies in England who approved of the new order after 1918, are also valuable, especially his *Racial Problems in Hungary* (Constable 1908); *The Southern Slav Question and the Habsburg Monarchy* (Constable 1911); *A History of the Rumanians* (Cambridge University Press 1934); and *A History of the Czechs and Slovaks* (Hutchinson 1943).

Library of the Twentieth Century will include the following titles:

Russia in Revolt
David Floyd
The Second Reich
Harold Kurtz
The Anarchists
Roderick Kedward
Suffragettes International
Trevor Lloyd
War by Time-Table
A.J.P. Taylor
Death of a Generation
Alistair Horne
Suicide of the Empires
Alan Clark
Twilight of the Habsburgs
Z.A.B. Zeman
Early Aviation
Sir Robert Saundby
Birth of the Movies
D.J. Wenden
Theodore Roosevelt
A.E. Campbell
Lenin's Russia
G. Katkov
The Weimar Republic
Sefton Delmer
Out of the Lion's Paw
Constantine Fitzgibbon
Japan: The Years of Triumph
Louis Allen
Communism Takes China
C.P. Fitzgerald
Black and White in South Africa
G.H. Le May
Woodrow Wilson
R.H. Ferrell
France 1918-34
W. Knapp
France 1934-40
A.N. Wahl
Mussolini's Italy
Geoffrey Warner
The Little Dictators
A. Polonsky
Viva Zapata
L. Bethell
The World Depression
Malcolm Falkus
Stalin's Russia
A. Nova
The Brutal Reich
Donald Watt
The Spanish Civil War
Raymond Carr
Munich: Czech Tragedy
K.G. Robbins

Z A B Zeman was born in Prague and was educated there and in Great Britain. He has taught history at the universities of London, Oxford, and St Andrews. His published works include *Germany and the Revolution in Russia, 1915-1918, The Break-up of the Habsburg Empire, 1914-1918, Nazi Propaganda* and *Prague Spring: a Report on Czechoslovakia 1968*

JM Roberts, General Editor of the *Library of the 20th Century*, is Fellow and Tutor in Modern History at Merton College, Oxford. He is also General Editor of Purnell's *History of the 20th Century* and Joint-Editor of the *English Historical Review*, and author of *Europe 1880-1945* in the Longman's History of Europe. He has been English Editor of the *Larousse Encyclopedia of Modern History*, has reviewed for *The Observer, New Statesman,* and *Spectator*, and given talks on the BBC

Library of the 20th Century

Editor: Jonathan Martin
Assistant Editor: Jenny Ashby
Designed by: Brian Mayers/ Germano Facetti
Designer: Henning Boehlke
Research: Mary Frances Facetti

Pictures selected from the following sources:

BPC Library 56 58 60 102
British Museum 10
Brussels Army Museum 97
Diagram 6 34 120
Fotoarchív SPB, Praha 116
Fotoarchív VHÚ, Praha 111
M.L. Guaita 6 12 16 27 39 75 77 79 80 97
Heeresgeschichtliches Museum, Vienna 36 62 66 89 99
Imperial War Museum 108
Eric Lessing – Magnum, Paris 68 72
Library of Congress, Washington, D.C. 70
Mansell Collection 19 20 40 46
Nationalbibliothek Bildarchiv, Vienna 9 16 23 27 29 37 39 42 50 56 73 80 94 119
Photographie Giraudon, Paris 14
Radio Times Hulton Picture Library 65 106
Roger Viollet 56 91
Snark International 44
Snark/Photothèque Laffont 115
Südd-Verlag, Munich 16 24 30 37 49 53 54 74 84 87 89 93 100 104 113 120
Tasiemka 4
Ullstein 9 37 74 83

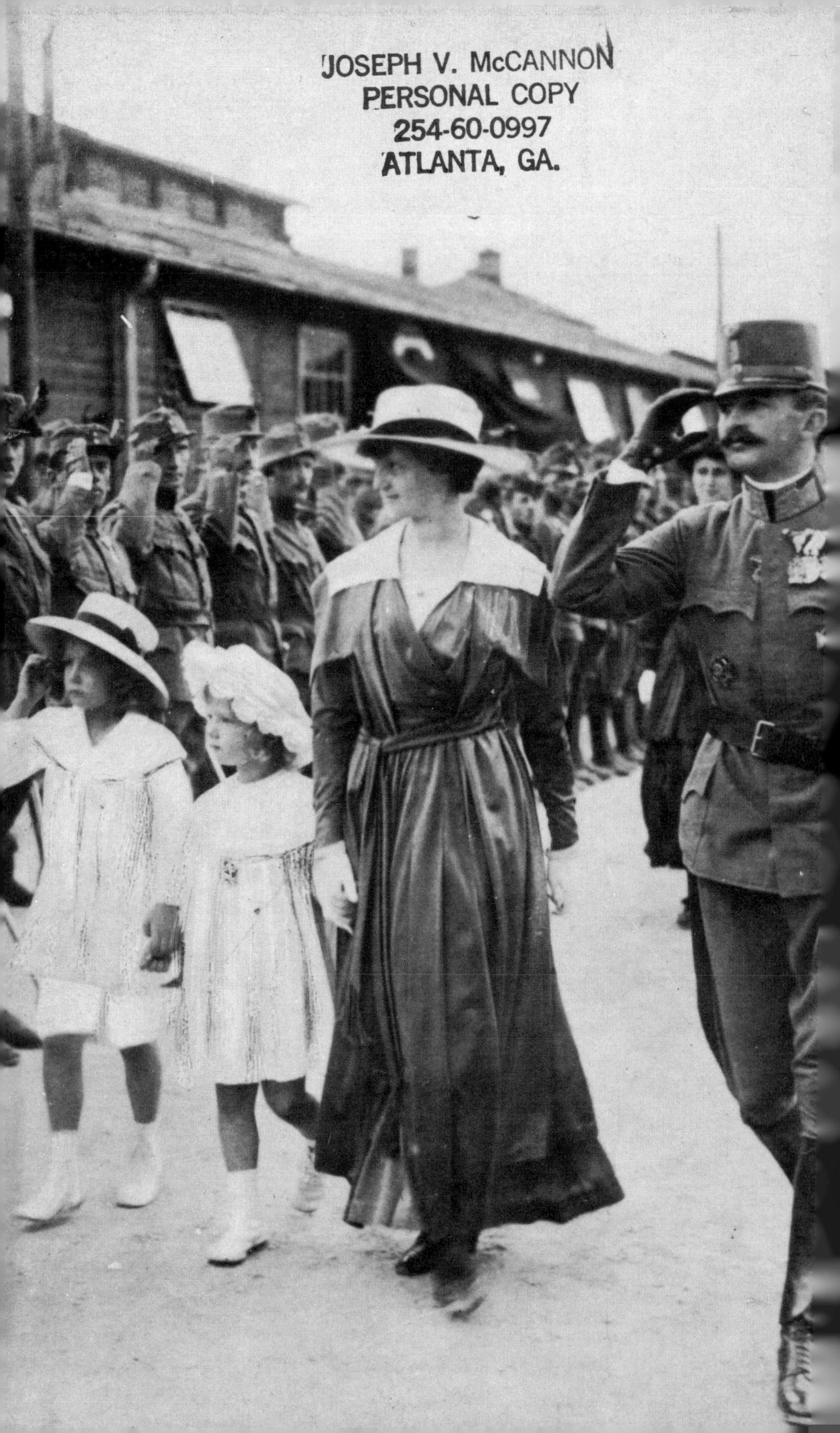